MINI
EDINBURGH

How to download your Free eBook

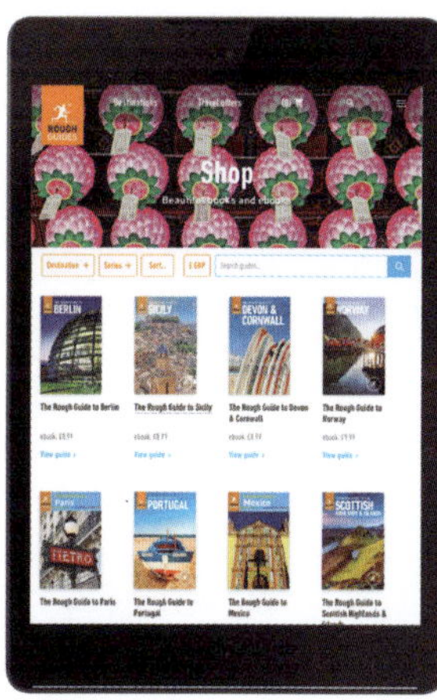

1. Visit **www.roughguides.com/free-ebook** or scan the **QR code** opposite

2. Enter the code **edinburgh334**
3. Follow the simple step-by-step instructions

For troubleshooting contact: mail@roughguides.com

Contents

Introduction

There is something fantastical about the setting of Scotland's capital city. Hemmed in by the Pentland Hills to the south and the waters of the Firth of Forth to the north, Edinburgh is an extraordinary urban centre encompassing chunks of wilderness, ramshackle medieval tenements, stately Georgian townhouses and a castle-topped ridge. Yet, one of the city's delights is that it is not simply a collection of heartless historic facades. It is instead a living, thriving community. The day-to-day lives of around half a million inhabitants are set against a rich backdrop of monuments, myths, martyrs and memories – those things which make Edinburgh such a magnet for visitors.

The view from Calton Hill

WHEN TO GO

Being closer to sunny East Lothian than the sodden west coast, Edinburgh's main climatic drawback is not so much precipitation as biting wind. Even in summer, sea breezes can keep temperatures down, as can the haar, mist that sometimes rolls in after a spell of fine weather. In recent years, March, April and May have seen some of the best and most prolonged spells of warm sunshine and blue skies (enhanced, in May at least, by wonderfully long days and short nights), though the implications for climate change are less than wonderful. The summer months of June, July and especially August (average max 17–19°) are notoriously unpredictable and often wet, as Fringe regulars know only too well. While winters are generally cold (average max 7–10°) and gloomy, you can still be lucky and hit upon a gorgeous few days of crisp sunshine. Crowds of tourists now throng Edinburgh year-round, reaching a peak during the Fringe, Christmas and especially New Year.

A tale of two cities

Edinburgh, like Rome, is built on seven hills, an area welded together by volcanic activity 350 million years ago. Rising 435ft (133 metres) above sea level is the Castle Rock, used for thousands of years as a vantage point for defensive strongholds.

The town became the 'principal burgh' of the kingdom during the reign of James III (1460–88), and in the following years it blossomed. Complete districts from that time are still in place, brimming with churches, taverns, tollhouses and tenements, or 'lands'. These tall buildings were crammed with family upon family, with the gentry and merchant classes below and the commoners above. They are crisscrossed with numerous narrow alleys, or 'wynds', which are separated by open spaces where markets were held, royal decrees announced, and criminals hanged in front of large, baying crowds.

Some three hundred years later, at the end of the eighteenth century, this medieval city witnessed the birth of a sibling. The

The Royal Mile

'New Town' became one of the most elegant Georgian cities in the world, still very much complete today.

Although Edinburgh ceased to be the political capital in 1707 (following the Act of Union, which saw Scotland united with England under one monarch and parliament in London), the city instead became a crucible of thought, home to pioneering philosophers, scientists, architects, engineers, painters and authors.

While the rich abandoned the ramshackle Old Town to the poor, flitting to the Neoclassical grandeur of the New Town, the nineteenth century also saw a city-wide boom in the middle classes, working in banking, insurance and law. Inspired by the economic doctrines of Adam Smith, lawyers and accountants made a fortune investing the wealth of Scottish industrialists in foreign ventures. Edinburgh continues to house one of the largest financial communities in Europe.

AULD REEKIE

In old Edinburgh almost every room was kept warm with an open fire, and sooty plumes rose daily above the city. Following the Industrial Revolution, factories and smoke-belching trains added to the problem. As a result, Edinburgh was given the nickname 'Auld Reekie' (Old Smoky).

National treasure

During the summer months Edinburgh's population trebles as tourists flood into the city to see the many national treasures contained within its boundaries. A large proportion will visit Edinburgh Castle, Scotland's most popular attraction and home to the Honours of Scotland (crown jewels). It formerly housed the Stone of Destiny (see pages 20 and 21), but the symbolic coronation seat is now on display in the 2024-opened Perth Museum in Perthshire.

Edinburgh shelters three branches of the National Galleries of Scotland – National, Portrait and Modern (spread across two collections, Modern One and Modern Two). You'll also find the Royal Palace of Holyroodhouse, one of the British royal family's most ancient residences. Edinburgh's major museums include the National Museum of Scotland, which documents the country's history from earliest times to the present day.

WHAT'S NEW

Whisky tourism is having a moment in Edinburgh. In 2021, Johnnie Walker Princes Street (www.johnniewalker.com) opened in the centre of the capital: an eight-storey Art Deco whisky emporium offering immersive tours, light shows and tastings. Over on the other side of the castle, the Scotch Whisky Experience (www.scotchwhiskyexperience.co.uk) has undergone a £3 million revamp. Further afield in Perthshire, the Glenturret distillery – a popular day-trip from the capital – was given a luxury spin by new Swiss owners Lalique in 2019, with experiential tours, a Michelin-starred restaurant and a boutique shop stocking a 50-year-old single malt for a bank-breaking £50,000. In 2023, for the first time in seventy years, trams rattled down Leith Walk on a new 5km, eight-stop route running from central Edinburgh north to Leith docks before stopping at its final destination Newhaven. Hop off at Leith to tour the new Port of Leith Distillery (www.leithdistillery.com) – the UK's first vertical distillery – and savour a dram overlooking the Firth of Forth.

SUSTAINABLE TRAVEL

One of the best ways to travel sustainably is to avoid flying or driving. The most satisfying way to reach, and travel around, Edinburgh, is by public transport. The capital is easily accessed by train from various parts of England, from where there are routes (some extraordinarily scenic) along the west and east coasts for those venturing further afield. Edinburgh is best explored on foot or by bike, both excellent zero-emission transport alternatives. While dining out in the city, consider going vegetarian or vegan to dodge the adverse environmental impacts of consuming meat. Seek out Edinburgh's *Seeds for the Soul* (www.seedsforthesoul.co.uk), whose nourishing bowls and burgers are quite the thing. For shopping, prioritise buying local. If you pick up produce and other goods at markets, you are buying direct from the seller, thereby cutting out many of the unsustainable practices associated with behemoth supermarkets. Stay in guesthouses and small independent hotels to line the pockets of locals as opposed to hospitality giants. Better still, look for sustainable stays, be it through green practices; zero-kilometre restaurants; or incentives for public transport.

Festival city

The people of Edinburgh have traditionally pursued such conservative, respectable vocations as banking, medicine, law and academia. But their wealth of earnest achievement doesn't mean they lack verve or the ability to enjoy themselves. The city's urbane residents enjoy their galleries, theatres and exhibitions as much as visitors do. Their restaurants are helmed by internationally renowned chefs who create dishes using some of the finest fish and meat in the world. Locals love to socialise, gathering in the hundreds of characterful pubs, bars and cafés.

Established by Sir Rudolph Bing in the wake of World War II, Edinburgh's annual arts festival aimed to attract major names in music, drama and dance. By 1987, the Edinburgh International

Festival had grown into the largest annual arts event in the world, with hundreds of performances in numerous venues across the city during August.

Today, the main arts festival is only part of a veritable circus of summer activities. Regiments of soldiers in full dress regalia march to the sound of pipe and drum in the Military Tattoo, and film connoisseurs gather for a key event in the international movie calendar. The Mela Festival is an infectious delight of world music and international dance held on Leith Links. However, the Festival Fringe is by far the most visible and most attended of Edinburgh's August Festivals. Another great time to visit Edinburgh is at the turn of the year, when the city hosts one of the world's biggest New Year's Eve parties.

Edinburgh is a city of contrasts: a historic UNESCO World Heritage Site on one hand; a lively modern city with a festival heart on the other. A flurry of investment saw the introduction of the tram system in 2014 (with extensions to Leith in 2023), followed by regeneration projects at St James Quarter and along Princes Street. The New Waverley development has provided the city with an eclectic mix of shops, cafés, restaurants and hotels. Centred around a row of renovated Victorian arches and a new public square, it seamlessly links Waverley Station with the Royal Mile.

Fringe performers

10 Things not to miss

1 **THE SCOTTISH PARLIAMENT**
One of Europe's most stunning and controversial modern buildings. See page 61.

2 **ST GILES CATHEDRAL**
Featuring beautiful stained-glass windows and an ornate twentieth-century chapel. See page 50.

3 **THE SCOTT MONUMENT**
A Gothic masterpiece. See page 73.

4 **ARTHUR'S SEAT**
Climb this hulking great rock for a fantastic view of the city. See page 61.

5 **EDINBURGH CASTLE**
Home of the Honours of Scotland and the One O'Clock Gun, and the site of the Military Tattoo. See page 39.

6 **CHARLOTTE SQUARE**
Located in Edinburgh's Georgian New Town, it is the finest square in the city. See page 76.

7 **FESTIVALS**
Every summer, visitors flock to the city for its world-leading festivals. See page 93.

8 **THE NATIONAL GALLERIES OF SCOTLAND: NATIONAL**
One of the best art collections in Europe. See page 66.

9 **THE NATIONAL MUSEUM OF SCOTLAND**
Telling the history of Scotland. See page 66.

10 **THE PALACE OF HOLYROODHOUSE**
The King's home in Scotland has ornate interiors and a long history. See page 56.

A perfect day in Edinburgh

8.30AM

Breakfast. The ideal place to start a day of culture is at the *Scottish Café* inside the National Galleries of Scotland: National, on Princes Street. Set yourself up with a traditional breakfast before a look around the gallery's world-class collection of pre-twentieth-century European art.

10AM

Edinburgh Castle. Follow the Mound, crossing Princes Street Gardens towards the Old Town, and climb the steep steps up to the castle. From this prime perch, you can take in some of the finest views across the New Town below.

11.30AM

Castle Hill. Walk back down Castle Hill, taking the time to explore the vennels and wynds as you meander along the sloping streets.

12.30PM

Shopping. Off George V Bridge, Victoria Street is peppered with specialist shops, well worth a browse. After, press onto the Grassmarket for lots of lunch options. Retrace your steps and continue to High Street, where St Giles Cathedral dominates.

2PM

Royal Mile. Continue down the Royal Mile, where you can take your pick from various tourist big-hitters; the Museum of Childhood, John Knox House, the Museum of Edinburgh and Canongate Tolbooth. Near the end of the road, the Scottish Parliament Building looms into view.

3PM

Holyroodhouse. At the foot of the Royal Mile, the Palace of Holyroodhouse stands sentinel. It is worth taking time to see the fine collection of royal artefacts (if the royal family are not in residence). Alternatively, if the weather allows, explore the sprawling Holyrood Park behind.

4PM

Afternoon tea. Walk back up the Royal Mile. Just past the Scottish Parliament is *Clarinda's Tearoom*, a great pitstop for home-baked treats.

7.30PM

Dinner. After freshening up at your hotel, head to the New Town – excellent restaurants cluster around George Street. For fine Italian cooking, try the ever-popular *Gusto* or *Contini*. If you're marking a special occasion, *Number One* is the place to go.

9.30PM

On the town. Warm up with a drink at the *Guildford Arms*, a traditional pub on West Register Street. Then, move on to George Street and pop into the *Lulu*, a trendy club beneath the *Tigerlily* hotel; or perhaps sip a Foxtrot Fizz or a Red Rum at *Bramble* in nearby Queen Street.

Budget Edinburgh

8AM

Breakfast. Pick up coffee and pastries from *Fortitude*, a small and friendly coffee bar and on-site roastery where the baristas really know their beans. More filling options include brunch dishes like avocado on sourdough toast, plus plenty of gluten-free and vegan options.

9AM

Old Calton Burial Ground. On Calton Hill's southern slopes, this atmospheric tangle of mausoleums and gravestones makes for an absorbing wander. Look out for the cylindrical memorial to one of Edinburgh's greatest sons, philosopher David Hume.

10AM

Scottish Poetry Library. Pop by this temple to poetry (see page 55) to discover native verse beyond the infamous Rabbie Burns. Try to spot the Mystery Book Sculptures, miniature artworks made from books and left anonymously in cultural centres across the city.

11AM

Museum of Childhood. Hark back to simpler times with a nostalgic deep dive into trains, games, dolls and hobbies designed to stoke the imagination of young minds. See page 53.

NOON

Museum of Edinburgh. Trace the history of the capital city in this labyrinth of wood-panelled rooms, one of which displays the original National Covenant, a petition for religious freedom drawn up on a deerskin parchment in 1638. See page 54.

1.30PM

Lunch. For budget eats, feast on Mexican *antojitos* (tapas-sized street food) at *El Cartel Casera Mexicana*. Pick from tacos, street corn and quesadillas, or more unusual options like baby-back pork ribs with a cumin, garlic and pineapple glaze.

3PM

General Register House. Pore over thousands of records dating back five hundred years in this distinguished building designed by Robert Adam. Trace your family tree in the Scotland's People Centre, a dedicated history unit for those researching genealogical records. See page 74.

5.30PM

St Mary's Cathedral. Catch the daily evensong and get in touch with your spiritual side beneath the glorious gothic arches.

7PM

Dinner. Make your way to *Mother India's Cafe* (3–5 Infirmary St) in the Old Town for tapas with a twist, so the restaurant slogan goes; the twist being that the food is Indian, not Spanish. Also, plenty of classics like *daal makhni* and chicken tikka on offer.

Haunted Edinburgh

8AM

Coffee. Grab an early-morning pick-me-up from *Artisan Roast* (57 Broughton St), an unstoppable force in the connoisseur coffee roasters' market. If your hotel is too far from the original, fear not: the sweet, nutty brews can be found in independent cafés all over town.

9AM

James V's Tower, Palace of Holyroodhouse. This haunted Edinburgh tour kicks off at the scene of a crime: the murder of Mary, Queen of Scots' secretary, David Rizzio. Look for what is supposedly the bloodstains still visible on the wooden floor. See page 59.

10.30AM

Surgeons' Hall Museums. A conspicuously ostentatious exterior belies one of Scotland's grisliest museums, whose collection ranges from early surgical tools to a pocketbook covered with the leathered skin of serial killer William Burke. From the eighteenth century, Edinburgh was a leading centre of medical and anatomical research, nurturing world-famous pioneers such as James Young Simpson, founder of anaesthesia, and Joseph Lister, the father of modern surgery. See page 67.

12.30PM

The Real Mary King's Close. If you haven't lost your appetite, grab a quick bite to eat at *Mussel Inn* (61–65 Rose St, http://mussel-inn.com), whose honest lunchtime offering includes a bowl of mussels or seafood chowder with fries for under £10. After, dodge the ghosts in Mary King's Close, a dank warren of subterranean tenements where plague victims were once entombed alive.

3PM

South Bridge Vaults. Home to a particularly unpleasant poltergeist, these notoriously creepy catacombs consistently take the honours as Edinburgh's most haunted.

4PM

Edinburgh Castle. Pick your way to the Witches Well (see page 46), where hundreds of women were burnt at the stake; some are reported to stalk the Castle corridors.

6PM

Dinner. Where else to dine after a hard day's ghost-hunting but amid the Gothic splendour of *The Witchery by the Castle* (see page 118)? Ask for a table in the secret garden.

7PM

Greyfriars Kirkyard. Run the gauntlet of the downright-dangerous McKenzie Poltergeist on a night-time tour into the depths of the Covenanter's Prison and Black Mausoleum. The kirkyard was known for grave-robbing as freshly interred bodies were exhumed and sold to the nearby medical school.

History

The city of Edinburgh grew up around the steep, ragged cliff of the Castle Rock and its easily defended summit. Archaeological excavations have revealed evidence of habitation here as long ago as 900 BC. Very little, however, is known about the Rock and its inhabitants in the centuries between its first occupation and the time of the MacAlpin kings. A few shadowy details have been left to us by the Romans and by an epic poem from the seventh century.

Romans and Britons

In AD 78–84 the Romans invaded Scotland where they met a group called the Picts, whom they drove north. They consolidated their gains by building the Antonine Wall across the waist of Scotland between the Firth of Forth and the River Clyde in about AD 150. Roman legions encountered the strongholds of the Castle Rock and Arthur's Seat, held by a tribe of ancient Britons – the Votadini. Little is known of them, but they were probably the ancestors of the Gododdin, whose feats are told in a seventh-century Old Welsh manuscript. Their capital, Din Eidyn, fell to the Angles in 638 and became part of the Anglian kingdom

Robert the Bruce

of Northumbria. It was the first of many times that the site would change hands.

> **NOTES**
>
> Din Eidyn (the 'Fort of Eidyn') – almost certainly the Castle Rock – was the Gododdin tribe's capital. The name lives on in the *Edin* of Edinburgh.

The MacAlpin kings

Four distinct peoples once inhabited the land now known as Scotland: the Picts in the north, the Britons in the southwest, the invading Angles in the southeast, and the Scots in the west. The Scots were Gaelic-speaking immigrants from the north of Ireland. Kenneth MacAlpin, who ruled as King of Scots at Dunadd, acquired the Pictish throne in 843, uniting Scotland north of the River Forth into a single kingdom. He moved his capital – along with the Stone of Destiny (on which Scottish kings were crowned) – to the sacred Pict site of Scone, close to Perth. His great-great-great-grandson, Malcolm II (1005–34), defeated the Angles at the Battle of Carham in 1018 and extended Scottish territory as far south as the River Tweed. These new lands included the stronghold of Edinburgh.

Malcolm II's grandson, Malcolm Canmore (1058–93), often visited Edinburgh with his wife Margaret, a Saxon princess. They crossed the Forth from Dunfermline at the narrows known to this day as Queensferry. Margaret was a deeply pious woman who was subsequently canonised, and her youngest son, David I (1124–53), founded a church in her name on the highest point of the Castle Rock (St Margaret's Chapel). David also founded the Abbey of Holyrood and created several royal burghs (towns with special trading privileges), including Edinburgh and Canongate; the latter was under the jurisdiction of the monks, or 'canons', of Holyrood.

At this point in time, Edinburgh was still a modest town, but David's successor, Malcolm IV (1153–65), made its castle his main residence. By the end of the twelfth century, Edinburgh's castle was used as a royal treasury. The town's High Street stretched from the castle along the ridge to the east (today the Royal Mile), past the parish church of St Giles, and out to the Netherbow, where Edinburgh ended and Canongate began.

Wars of independence

In 1286 the MacAlpin dynasty ended, leaving Scotland without a ruler. There were a number of claimants to the throne, among them John Balliol, Lord of Galloway, and Robert de Brus, Lord of Annandale. The guardians of Scotland were unable to decide who should succeed and asked the English king, Edward I, to adjudicate. Edward, seeing this invitation as a chance to assert his claim as overlord of Scotland, chose John Balliol, whom he judged to be the weaker of the two.

Edward treated King John as a vassal. However, when Edward went to war with France in 1294 and summoned John along with other knights, the Scottish king decided he had had enough. He ignored Edward's summons and instead negotiated a treaty with the French king, the beginning of a long association between France and Scotland that would become known as the 'Auld Alliance'.

Edward was furious and his reprisal was swift and bloody. In 1296 he led a force of nearly 30,000 men into Scotland and captured the castles of Roxburgh, Edinburgh and Stirling. The Stone of Destiny and the Scottish crown jewels were stolen, and Scotland's Great Seal was broken up. Oaths of fealty were demanded from Scottish nobles, while English officials were installed to oversee the running of the country. Scotland became little more than an English county.

NOTES

When in power, Robert the Bruce was so concerned by the ease with which the English could advance on Edinburgh and dominate the country from the Castle that he demolished it, except for the small chapel of St Margaret.

But the Scots did not take this insult lying down. Bands of rebels (such as those led by William Wallace) began to attack the English garrisons and make raids into English territory. When Wallace was captured, the Scots looked for a new leader and discovered one in Robert the Bruce, grandson of the Robert de Brus rejected by Edward in 1292. He was crowned King of Scots at Scone in 1306 and began his campaign to drive the English out of Scotland.

A fifteenth-century illumination of St Margaret

Edward I died in 1307 and was succeeded by his son, Edward II, who in 1314 led an army of 25,000 men to confront Bruce's army at Bannockburn, near Stirling. Though outnumbered, the Scots sent the English packing. Robert the Bruce continued to harass the English until they were forced to sue for peace. A truce was declared, and the Treaty of Northampton was negotiated at Edinburgh in 1328.

Although many Scottish nobles were dedicated to the cause of independence, others either bore grudges against the ruling king or held lands in England that they feared to lose. These divisions – later hardened by religious schism – would forever deny Scotland a truly united voice.

When Robert the Bruce died in 1329, his son and heir, David II, was only five years old. Within a few years the wars with England resumed, aggravated by civil war at home as Edward Balliol (son of

Mons Meg – a gift to James IV from the Duke of Burgundy

John) tried to take the Scottish throne with the help of the English king, Edward III.

The Stewart dynasty

During these stormy years, the castle of Edinburgh was occupied several times by English garrisons. In 1341 it was taken from the English by William of Douglas. The young David II returned from exile in France and made it his principal royal residence, building a tower house (David's Tower) on the site of what is now the Half Moon Battery. He died in 1371 and was succeeded by his nephew, Robert II. David's sister Marjory had married Walter the Steward, and their son was the first of the long line of Stewart (later spelt *Stuart*) monarchs who would reign over Scotland – and, subsequently, Great Britain – until the 'Glorious Revolution' of 1688.

The strength and wealth of Scotland increased during the reigns of the first Stewart kings. Castles were built and weapons acquired, including the gun, 'Mons Meg'. Edinburgh emerged as Scotland's main political centre and was declared by James III (1460–88) to be 'the principal burgh of our kingdom'.

James IV (1488–1513) confirmed Edinburgh's status as the capital of Scotland by constructing a royal palace at Holyrood. He cemented a peace treaty with England by marrying Margaret Tudor, daughter of Henry VII – the so-called Marriage of the Thistle and the Rose – but this did not prevent him from making a raid into England in 1513. The attack culminated in the Battle of Flodden, near the River Tweed, where the king was killed. Fearing invasion, the Edinburgh town council built a wall (the 'Flodden Wall') around the city boundaries.

Yet again a child – the infant James V – succeeded to the throne, and Scottish nobles were divided as to whether Scotland should draw closer to England or seek help from her old ally, France. The adult James leant towards France and in 1537 took a French wife, Mary of Guise. She bore two sons who both died in infancy, but by the time she was about to give birth to their third child, her husband lay dying at Falkland

Heraldic panel for James V at Holyroodhouse

Palace. On 8 December 1542 a messenger arrived with news that the queen had produced a daughter at the palace of Linlithgow. A few days later the king was dead, leaving a week-old baby girl to inherit the Scottish crown.

Mary, Queen of Scots

At the age of nine months, the baby Mary Stuart was crowned Queen of Scots at the Chapel Royal, Stirling. When the news reached London, Henry VIII saw his chance to subdue Scotland again and negotiated a marriage between the infant Mary and his son Edward. The Scots refused, and Henry sent an army rampaging through Scotland on a campaign known as the 'Rough Wooing'. The English king ordered his general to 'burn Edinburgh town so there may remain forever a perpetual memory of the vengeance of God lightened upon the Scots'.

Mary, Queen of Scots, depicted on the Great Tapestry of Scotland

But more was at stake than simply Scotland's independence: there was now a religious schism within Britain. In order to divorce Catherine of Aragon and marry Anne Boleyn, Henry VIII had broken with Rome and brought the English church under his own control. England was thus now a Protestant country, caught between Catholic France and the Scots with their new Catholic queen.

> **NOTES**
>
> A recurring feature of Scottish history is the inheritance of the throne by a child. Mary Stuart was just six days old when she succeeded James V.

The Scots themselves were divided, many embracing Protestantism while others remained staunchly Catholic. However, fear of the rampaging English army led the Scots again to seek help from their old allies in France, and the young queen married the Dauphin François, son of the French king.

François II became king of France in 1559 but died soon after. In 1561 the 18-year-old Mary returned to a Scotland in the grip of the Reformation, as Protestant leaders had taken control of the Scottish Parliament and abolished the authority of the pope. Her Protestant cousin, Elizabeth Tudor, was on the English throne, but Elizabeth – the 'Virgin Queen' – had no heir. Mary was next in line for the English crown, and Elizabeth suspected her intentions.

The six years of Mary's reign were turbulent ones. She clashed early on with Edinburgh's Protestant reformer, John Knox, who held sway in St Giles, but later adopted an uneasy policy of religious tolerance. In 1565 she married her young cousin Henry, Lord Darnley, much to the chagrin of Elizabeth (Darnley was a grandson of Margaret Tudor and thus also had a claim to the English throne). On 19 June 1566, in Edinburgh Castle, Mary gave birth to a son, Prince James.

Within a year, however, Darnley was murdered. Mary immediately immersed herself in controversy by marrying the Earl of Bothwell, the chief suspect. Mary was forced to abdicate in 1567, and the infant prince was crowned as James VI.

Mary sought asylum in England, only to be imprisoned by Elizabeth. The English queen kept her cousin in captivity for twenty years and finally had her beheaded on a trumped-up charge of treason. So it was bitterly ironic when Elizabeth died without

James VI of Scotland who became James I of England

an heir and James, Mary's Catholic son, inherited the English throne.

In 1603 James VI of Scotland was thus crowned James I of England, marking the Union of the Crowns. Although Scotland was still a separate kingdom, the two countries would from that day be ruled by the same monarch.

The Covenanters

The population of Edinburgh grew fast between 1500 and 1650, and a maze of tall, unsanitary tenements sprouted along the spine of the High Street. The castle was extended, and in 1582 the Town's College (the precursor of the University of Edinburgh) was founded. James died in 1625, and was succeeded by his son, Charles I, who proved an incompetent ruler. In 1637 his attempt to force the Scottish Presbyterian Church into accepting an English liturgy and the rule of bishops led to civil revolt and rioting.

The next year, a large group of Scottish churchmen and nobles signed the National Covenant, pledging allegiance to the Presbyterian faith. At first, the so-called Covenanters sided with Oliver Cromwell's Parliamentarians in the civil war that had erupted across the border. But when the English revolutionaries beheaded Charles I in 1649, the Scots rallied round his son, Charles II. Cromwell's forces invaded Scotland, crushed the Covenanters and went on to take Edinburgh. Scotland suffered ten years of military rule under Cromwell's Commonwealth.

Scotland's troubles continued after Charles II's restoration to the throne in 1660. The Covenanters faced severe persecution at the hands of the king's supporters, who had decided to follow his father's policy of imposing bishops on the Scots. Hundreds of Covenanters were imprisoned and executed.

In the end England underwent the 'Glorious Revolution' of 1688, when Catholic James II (Scotland's James VII) was deposed and the Protestant William of Orange (1689–1702) took the British crown. Presbyterianism was established as Scotland's official state church and the Covenanters prevailed.

Act of Union

On 1 May 1707 England and Scotland were formally joined together by the 'Act of Union' – establishing the Union of Parliaments – and the United Kingdom was born. Although Scotland retained its own legal system, education system and national Presbyterian Church, the move was opposed by the majority of Scots. The supporters of the deposed James VII and his successors, exiled in France, were known as the 'Jacobites'. Several times during the next 40 years they tried to restore the Stuart dynasty to the British throne, though by this time the crown had passed to the German House of Hanover. James Edward Stuart, known as the 'Old Pretender', travelled up the Firth of Forth in 1708 but was driven back by British ships and bad weather. Another campaign was held in 1715 under the Jacobite Earl of Mar, but it was the 1745 rising of Prince Charles Edward Stuart, the 'Young Pretender', which became the stuff of legend.

The prince, known as Bonnie Prince Charlie the grandson of James VII), raised an army of Jacobite Highlanders and swept through Scotland. They occupied Edinburgh (but not the castle) and defeated a government army at the Battle of Prestonpans. In

Robert Burns

November of that year he invaded England, capturing Carlisle and driving south as far as Derby, only 125 miles (200km) short of London.

Finding his forces outnumbered and overextended here, the young prince beat a tactical retreat, but the English army hounded him relentlessly. The final showdown – at Culloden in 1746 – saw the Jacobite army slaughtered. Prince Charlie fled and was pursued over the Highlands before escaping in a French ship. He died in Rome in 1788, disillusioned and drunk.

Scottish Enlightenment

The Jacobite uprisings found little support in such Lowland cities as Edinburgh. Here there was a growing sense that the Union was around to stay. Within ten years of the Young Pretender's occupation of Holyrood, the town council of Edinburgh proposed a plan to relieve the chronic overcrowding of the Royal Mile tenements by constructing a New Town on land north of the castle. In 1767 a design by a young architect, James Craig, was approved and work began.

This architectural renaissance in Edinburgh was followed by an intellectual flowering in the sciences, philosophy and medicine that revolutionised Western society in the late eighteenth century. Famous Edinburgh residents of this period – later known as the

Scottish Enlightenment – included David Hume, eminent British philosopher and author of *A Treatise of Human Nature*, pioneering economist Adam Smith, author of *The Wealth of Nations*, and scientist Joseph Black, who discovered the concept of latent heat. Robert Burns' poems and Walter Scott's novels rekindled interest in Scotland's history and nationhood.

The modern city

In the nineteenth century Edinburgh was swept up in the Industrial Revolution. The coalfields of Lothian and Fife fuelled the growth of baking, distilling, printing and machine-making industries. Smoke from factories gave rise to Edinburgh's nickname, 'Auld Reekie'. With the arrival of the railways in the mid-1800s, the city grew as new lines led to the spread of suburbs.

During the twentieth century Edinburgh built and consolidated its position as a European centre of finance, learning and culture.

BURKE AND HARE

In the early nineteenth century, Edinburgh was at the forefront of the medical world, making great strides in the understanding of diseases and infections. As part of this research process, the medical establishment needed cadavers for dissection, and a grisly black market developed, headed by William Burke and William Hare. At first they earned their money by digging up freshly buried corpses to sell to physicians, but when demand outstripped supply, they began to roam the streets around the Grassmarket looking for suitable victims, whom they lured into dark alleyways and strangled.

Only when Hare testified in court against his partner was the unsavoury business brought to the public eye. Genteel society was outraged. Hare got away with his nefarious deeds, but Burke was hanged in the Grassmarket in 1829 and his body used for medical research.

The rise of the Edinburgh International Festival and the extraordinary growth of the Fringe around it, set against a rich backdrop of architecture and history, established the city as one of the top tourist destinations in the UK.

Edinburgh never ceased to think of itself defiantly as the nation's capital and the latter part of the twentieth century saw a concerted (though peaceful) effort to gain self-determination for Scotland. In 1979 the nationalists were in disarray when a referendum was defeated. Further efforts came to nought during the following years of Conservative rule at Westminster, although the Stone of Destiny was returned to Scottish soil in 1996 – seven hundred years after it had been taken south by the English.

The election of New Labour in 1997 was a turning point in history. The new government organised a referendum on Scottish devolution and a majority voted for the creation of a Scottish Parliament. Political power returned to Edinburgh after nearly three hundred years. The new Parliament opened July 1999 and in October 2004 it moved to a state-of-the-art building at Holyrood. This seat of power, however, remained affiliated to Westminster after another defeated bid for independence in the 2014 referendum, despite the Scottish Parliament gaining more devolutionary powers. Having lost the argument for independence, some predicted the demise of the SNP.

Yet, despite the resignation of Alex Salmond, the SNP came out on top, with Nicola Sturgeon – the extremely popular new leader – sweeping the boards in all but one of the Scottish Westminster constituencies in the 2015 general election – a record never before achieved by any party.

The 2016 Holyrood elections saw Scotland's political landscape change again, leaving SNP just shy of an outright majority and the Conservatives in second place. The Brexit referendum revealed a fragmented UK, with 52 percent of voters opting to leave the EU, though in Scotland 62 percent voted to remain. Come the 2019 general elections, the Scottish National Party went from strength to strength, securing 48 of the fifty available seats, at the expense of both Labour and Conservative.

After Scotland dealt with the Covid-19 pandemic well, certainly in comparison to their English counterparts, Nicola Sturgeon stirred up surprise when she resigned as First Minister in 2023. She was replaced by Humza Yousaf, the first Muslim to lead a major UK party. However, little more than a year after taking up office, Yousaf resigned following the collapse of the SNP's powersharing deal with the Greens.

Veteran politician John Swinney took the reins, but far worse was to come for the SNP when the party lost 39 of their 48 seats

First Minister John Swinney

Greyfriars Bobby statue with a mask during the Covid-19 pandemic

in the general election as both Labour and the Liberal Democrats made massive gains – voters sought to punish the party over disillusionment over a lack of progress towards independence, internal divisions over gender reform, and ongoing police investigations into party finances, among other things. Their task now is to regroup ahead of the Scottish Parliamentary elections in 2026.

Chronology

900 BC Late-Bronze/early-Iron Age settlement on Castle Rock.
1st–2nd centuries AD Roman occupation of southern Scotland; hill fort of the Votadini tribe on Castle Rock.
843 Scotland north of the Forth united under Kenneth MacAlpin.
1124–53 Reign of David I, founder of Abbey of Holyrood.
1297 Scots rebels under Wallace defeat English at Stirling Bridge.

1314 Scots victory under Robert the Bruce at Bannockburn.
1513 Scots suffer defeat at Flodden; Edinburgh builds city walls.
1544 The Rough Wooing: Henry VIII's forces sack Edinburgh.
1559–72 John Knox is minister of St Giles.
1560 Protestantism is established as Scotland's national faith.
1561–7 Mary, Queen of Scots, lives in Holyrood Palace.
1603 Union of the Crowns: James VI of Scotland becomes James I of England.
1638 The National Covenant is signed at Greyfriars Kirkyard.
1689 William of Orange invited to take over government of Scotland; civil war between William and Jacobites.
1707 'Act of Union' and creation of the UK; Scottish Parliament dissolved.
1745 Jacobite uprising; Bonnie Prince Charlie's army occupies Holyrood.
1767 Construction of Edinburgh's New Town begins.
1890 Forth Bridge opens.
1947 The first Edinburgh International Festival.
1995 Edinburgh's Old and New Towns become a UNESCO World Heritage Site.
1997 Referendum on Scottish devolution receives a majority vote.
1999 Scottish elections held; first 'new' Parliament opens 1 July.
2004 Opening of the iconic Parliament Building, stirring divided opinion among locals.
2008 The pro-independence Scottish National Party (SNP) becomes the largest party in the Scottish Parliament.
2014 Edinburgh votes to stay in the Union in a national referendum.
2020–22 Tourism seriously affected by Covid-19 pandemic, but after a successful vaccination programme, restrictions are eased, and visitor numbers slowly increase.
2024 The Scottish National Party loses 39 seats in general election. Former First Minister Alex Salmond dies at the age of 69.

The Canongate Tolbooth

Places

Edinburgh is a city of several distinct historical districts that are all eminently walkable. You can divide your visit into three or four separate itineraries, each of which could fill either an afternoon or an entire day. There are also bus tours around the city to help you get your bearings before you visit the attractions. Tour buses stand in line on Waverley Street opposite the main railway station (see page 133).

The Old Town

Highlights

- **Edinburgh Castle**, see page 39
- **The Royal Mile**, see page 45
- **Holyrood**, see page 55

Although no one can be certain how old the settlement of Edinburgh actually is, it is possible that people have been living there for over five thousand years. Even before that, the site of Edinburgh's **Old Town** has its own fascinating story to tell in terms of its geological origin. The Castle Rock and Arthur's Seat are the remains of lava streams that hardened after the two volcanoes around them became dormant and cold.

During the last Ice Age, huge glaciers covered the region, moving west to east across the land and gouging trenches on either side of the volcanic mounds. They resisted the great power of the ice and caused a long stream of sediment to collect. At the end of the Ice Age (some 13,000 years ago), the glaciers melted, leaving a long ridge of sediment sloping gradually from the top of the volcanic hills.

The original city of Edinburgh grew from the tiny community that first clung to the ridge, reaching down in a ribbon of development towards the Abbey of Holyrood, at the foot of the hill in the east. In the sixteenth century, the Flodden Wall – now almost completely destroyed – protected the population. Combined with the geological setting of the city, the wall stifled development. Instead of expanding outwards, the city had no choice but to grow upwards.

And so, Edinburgh's famous tenements (or 'lands') began to be built. At least six storeys high, they were reached through narrow alleys called 'closes' or 'wynds' that became the focus of city life. A constant cycle of building, decay, collapse and rebuilding – plus the occasional catastrophic fire – gave the Old Town its characteristic irregular layout and chimney-strewn skyline.

The Gate House of Edinburgh Castle

Edinburgh Castle

With steep, defendable sides and strategic vantage points, the site of Edinburgh Castle was contested for hundreds of years by generations of Picts, Scots, Britons and Angles. Dominating the skyline, the dramatically rising cliff of black basalt stone made the castle impregnable to all but the most wily commander. It was the seat of power for anyone who ruled the region, although it was not until the eleventh century that Edinburgh settled down to become the capital of an independent Scotland, with a royal residence constructed within the castle walls.

> **NOTES**
>
> A gun weighing 6.6 tons (6,040kg), Mons Meg was a gift to James II in 1457 from his wife's uncle, Philip the Good, Duke of Burgundy. Manufactured in Mons (now in Belgium), the gun was state-of-the-art for the time, but weighed so much that it could be transported only 3 miles (5km) per day; often the fighting had ended before it could be brought into play.

After the 'Act of Union' with England in 1707, the castle lost its strategic importance. Much of the present-day complex dates from the eighteenth and nineteenth centuries when the royal castle was transformed into a garrison fortress with barracks and modern defences. The Victorians, who had a penchant for reworking the history and legends of Scotland, also added romantic, neo-Gothic touches.

Today **Edinburgh Castle ❶** (www.edinburghcastle.scot) is one of the most popular attractions in Scotland. A visit to the castle will take at least two hours, and most people take advantage of the audio guide (for a small extra fee).

Your first view of the castle will be the **Gate House**, which you pass through to reach the inner wards. Built between 1886 and 1888, the structure was a Victorian attempt to recapture the medieval castle style, although it was more decorative than defensive.

Firing of the One O'Clock Gun

The dry ditches in front, however, date from the 1650s. In the 1920s, bronze statues of two Scottish heroes – William Wallace and Robert the Bruce – were added to the facade.

Once inside, you will find yourself in the lower ward, the area of the castle that has been most heavily bombarded in many military campaigns. The Old Guard House houses one of three gift shops in the castle grounds. The walkway here once had a ditch and drawbridge to protect the inner gate, called **Portcullis Gate**, which was reconstructed in the late sixteenth century on fourteenth-century foundations. It was the main entrance to the castle and a formidable obstacle to the enemy.

Passing through Portcullis Gate, you enter the middle ward of the castle. Ahead to your right is the **Argyll Battery**, with a line of muzzle-loading 18lb guns pointing out northwards over the skyline of the New Town (a prime spot for spectacular photos). To your left are the Lang Stairs, which lead up to the medieval castle. Walk along past the battery to the Cart Shed, built in the aftermath of the Jacobite uprising in 1746. It now houses a café but was originally used to store the provisions carts. Beside the café is Mills Mount Battery, the location of the **One O'Clock Gun**, fired at 1pm daily except Sunday, Good Friday and Christmas Day. Be prepared, for it is indeed noisy.

The cobbled street winds steeply upwards, past the Governor's House and the New Barracks, where you will find the **National War Museum** and the **Regimental Museum of the Royal Scots Dragoon Guards** (check online for opening hours). Eventually you will reach **Foog's Gate** – the name and age of the gate remain a source of debate – to enter the upper ward and the oldest parts of the castle. To the left is a gift shop, and directly ahead is tiny **St Margaret's Chapel**, said to have been built by David I in the early twelfth century in honour of his mother, Queen Margaret, who died in 1093. It is the oldest building in Edinburgh and is still the site of weddings and baptisms. Although the chapel has been renovated since its construction, you will find a wonderful example of a Romanesque arch in the interior. The stained-glass windows, one featuring a likeness of Margaret, were inserted into the existing openings in the 1920s. Just outside the entrance is the Mons Meg gun.

In an open area south of the chapel is the **Half-Moon Battery**, built on the site of David's Tower, which was once the largest and most formidable structure in the castle. Begun in 1368, it was the main royal lodging for centuries until it was left a wreck during the 'Lang Siege' of 1571–3.

Crown Square

At the very pinnacle of the upper ward is **Crown Square**, a beautiful collection of buildings housing the treasures of Scotland. On your right as you enter the square is the **Scottish National War**

Armour in the Great Hall

Memorial, the highest building in the city. The building was originally a barracks but was suitably refurbished by Sir Robert Lorimer in 1923 to commemorate the Scots who fell in World War I; the halls of remembrance also commemorate those who died in World War II and all other conflicts. Inside, there are leather-bound regimental books with each serviceperson's name duly inscribed. Splendidly ornate stone friezes depict battle scenes of World War I, with each branch of the forces represented.

Opposite the memorial is the **Great Hall**, built in 1503 for the wedding reception of James IV and the English Margaret Tudor. It was later used as the ceremonial and legislative chamber. The original hammer-beam wooden roof is the highlight of the design, with thick beams and painted decorations. Note the monogram of James – *IR4* – on some of the stone brackets, along with the red rose and the thistle signifying the new alliance of Scotland and England. The hall was used as a barracks through much of its later history before being renovated in 1887. The interior decor says much more about the Victorians' romantic image of Scotland than it does about how the room would have really looked.

On the west side of the square is the **Queen Anne Building**, with a café for lunch or afternoon tea. Also here is the entrance to the **Prison of War Exhibition** in the Castle Vaults, which explores the experiences of sailors of various nationalities who were incarcerated in the castle, having been captured during the Seven Years' War (1756–63), the American War of Independence (1776–83) and the Napoleonic Wars (1793–1815). The POWs' living quarters are recreated, with cramped cots and hammocks, and there are original prison doors graffitied by the prisoners.

Along the east side of Crown Square is the **Royal Palace**, home to the crown jewels of Scotland. The palace, much altered over the generations, was generally used as a residence only at times of dynastic importance or danger, when Holyrood, down in the lowland, was difficult to defend. On 19 June 1566 Mary Stuart gave birth to her son James (the future James VI of Scotland and James I of England) in the small antechamber off a larger room known as **Queen Mary's Room**. The last monarch to stay in the palace was Charles I, in 1633.

On the upper floors (once the royal chambers) there is an exhibition telling the story of the **Honours of Scotland**. These crown jewels are said to be the oldest complete set – crown, sceptre and sword – in Europe, unchanged since 1640. They lie on blue velvet in a secure glass cabinet in the Crown Room. The Scottish crown

EDINBURGH MILITARY TATTOO

In 1950 the city established a Military Tattoo at the same time as the Festival, and the two have now become an inseparable combination. The tattoo is a highly polished show of military marching, pageantry, mock battles and horsemanship, accompanied by the sounds of pipe-and-drum bands from around the world. All this happens nightly (except Sunday) against the backdrop of the magnificently floodlit castle in an arena erected in the Esplanade. Tickets (which sell out months in advance) can be bought over the counter from the Tattoo Ticket Sales Office at 1–3 Cockburn Street, by telephone or online (tel: 0131 225 1188; www.edintattoo.co.uk).

was fashioned of gold mined in Scotland, greatly embellished during the reign of Scotland's James III (1460–88). The sceptre and sword were each papal gifts – the former in 1494 and the latter in 1507; these reinforced the links between Scotland and Rome. Following union with England in 1707, however, there was little use for the Scottish regalia. They were locked in a trunk in a sealed room in Edinburgh Castle for 111 years before Sir Walter Scott received permission to open the room in 1818.

Next to the regalia formerly stood the **Stone of Destiny**, until it was moved to the newly opened Perth Museum in 2024, thus returning to Perthshire for the first time in over seven hundred years. The artifact historically served as the seat on which Scottish kings were crowned, a symbol of the land over which they would rule. In 1296 the stone was captured by the English from Scone Abbey and taken to London. It has been used during crowning ceremonies for all English (then British) monarchs ever since, sitting under the coronation throne. In 1996 the stone was returned to Scotland, though it will continue to make the journey to London's Westminster Abbey for every royal coronation.

On the lower floor of the Royal Palace, **Laich Hall** has been restored as closely as possible to its 1617 decor, using traditional techniques and colours. This was where the monarch met advisers and diplomats. Leaving the castle, you will walk across the **Esplanade**, a broad open area originally created for regimental drill practice. Today, it is usually used as a car park, but it offers superb views of both Princes Street to the north and the Old Town to the south. In summer the Esplanade is filled by a temporary arena for Military Tattoo performances and occasional music concerts.

NOTES

It is certainly worthwhile exploring the narrow closes (also known as wynds) that branch off the Royal Mile and retain centuries-old features.

Deacon Brodie's Tavern

The Royal Mile

The town of Edinburgh eventually spreads out below the castle, with a main street leading out the entrance and down to the Palace of Holyroodhouse. In the sixteenth century this thoroughfare became known as the **Royal Mile** because it was the route used by royalty to make their way from the castle to Holyrood. A mile long, the city's oldest thoroughfare comprises four sections: Castlehill, Lawnmarket, the High Street and the Canongate. In former times it even crossed the old outer boundary of Edinburgh before it reached the palace.

Since the route has never seen major redevelopment, it has grown haphazardly but organically over the centuries. Some buildings date from the sixteenth century, but it is also lined with buildings of almost every era, including numerous seventeenth- and eighteenth-century tenements sometimes thirteen storeys high.

These were the residential areas of the city, considered desirable when first built. Later, they were often home to many large families, rife with overcrowding and unsanitary conditions.

Before you leave the castle's Esplanade, look out for the small bronze fountain on the wall to the left of the entrance. This is the **Witches Well**, which marks the spot where, between 1479 and 1722, women condemned for practising black magic were burned at the stake.

Beyond the Esplanade you enter the first section of the Royal Mile, narrow, cobbled **Castlehill**. On your left you will find the **Tartan Weaving Mill** (www.thetartanweavingmill.co.uk), where you can follow the journey of wool from the sheep to the finished product. You can watch a tartan pattern being woven by machine and then choose from around 170 tartans in the shop. There are also gift shops selling quality Scottish products, such as Aran wool and silver jewellery. Built in 1850, the building itself was at one time the major water-storage facility for the New Town.

Camera Obscura and World of Illusions

Next to the weaving centre, across narrow Ramsay Lane, are the **Camera Obscura and World of Illusions** ❷ (www.camera-obscura.co.uk), set high above the tenement chimney stacks. A series of lenses and prisms projects a live

WHERE TO SHOOT THE BEST PICTURES

It is near-impossible to find another capital city in such a striking setting as Edinburgh: perched on a series of extinct volcanoes and rocky crags which rise from the generally flat landscape of the Lothians, with the sheltered shoreline of the Firth of Forth to the north.

From the summit of Calton Hill, the Old Town appears as an unforgettable vista of tightly packed tenements and spires that rise to the immense castle. Set up your tripod from this prime perch and get snapping. For a close-up of the medieval Old Town, duck inside the labyrinth of tortuous alleys and tightly packed closes. To capture the city in all its festival frenzy, visit in July when actors, comedians, artists, writers and celebs converge en masse for the world's biggest arts gathering.

And, of course, you can't photograph the Scottish capital without capturing Holyrood Park and its iconic natural wonder: the 823ft-high Arthur's Seat. Climb to the peak of the largest (and most impressive) of the city's volcanoes for fine views of the city and the Firth. Plus, with its untamed moors and sheer cliffs, the park itself is studded with vantage points from which to capture fine photos of a more wild Edinburgh.

image of the city onto a concave viewing screen inside the camera. It was built in the 1850s, when cameras were the height of fashion. Several people at one time can sit inside and watch the city at work. The experience is best when the weather is bright. There is a viewing platform around the camera, allowing first-hand viewing of the cityscape, including close-ups of stonework not otherwise possible to view. Visit the Camera Obscura first thing in the morning or later in the evening when it is at its quietest and the rooftop views are at their most impressive.

Across the road you'll find the **Scotch Whisky Experience** ❸ (www.scotchwhiskyexperience.co.uk), which tells the story of the development of Scottish whisky. The various tours naturally all

The Writers' Museum holds relics of three famed authors

include a chance to taste this complex drink and end with a barrel ride that whisks you through three hundred years of the 'water of life'. Visitors can also buy whisky – over three hundred varieties are available.

At the bottom of Castlehill, where the road meets Johnston Terrace, is the old, soot-black Tolbooth Kirk (or church), which has the highest steeple in the city at 239ft (73 metres). In the late 1990s the church underwent a massive renovation and was re-christened **The Hub**, acting as the permanent centre and offices for the Edinburgh International Festival, with a box office (see page 139), home to the Edinburgh International Festival offices. Although the venue is closed to the public for most of the year, the front terrace is open for folk to partake in refreshments while overlooking the Royal Mile.

Lawnmarket

Beyond the Hub, the Royal Mile is known as Lawnmarket. This was once the commercial centre of the Old Town, including a weekly fabric market. There are several old lands found down the narrow wynds leading off the main street. **Gladstone's Land** ❹ (www.nts.org.uk/visit/places/gladstones-land), once the home of a wealthy seventeenth-century merchant, still has a period shopfront, and inside it is authentically furnished to give an impression of life three hundred years ago. It also includes a gift shop with an array of merchandise on offer.

Behind Gladstone's Land is Lady Stair's Close, which leads to Lady Stair's House, home to the **Writers' Museum** ❺ (www.edinburghmuseums.org.uk; free). The beautifully renovated house (dating from 1622) contains manuscripts and personal effects from three of Scotland's best-known authors: Robert Burns, Sir Walter Scott and Robert Louis Stevenson. The Stevenson exhibition on the lower floor is particularly interesting, with photographs of the author travelling around the world before his untimely death at the age of 44 in Samoa. A room on the top floor holds temporary exhibitions about other writers and literary themes.

Next to the Writers' Museum is **James Court**. The philosopher David Hume lived here and was regularly visited by the economist

A SPLIT PERSONALITY

When Robert Louis Stevenson wrote *The Strange Case of Dr Jekyll and Mr Hyde* in 1886, it shocked genteel society. Little did people realise that although he set the book in London, he had based his story on the real-life case of an Edinburgh man.

Deacon William Brodie was a respectable cabinetmaker and locksmith who, when he closed his shop in the evening, lived another life. After dark he frequented the less respectable parts of town – gambling, cockfighting and fathering five illegitimate children. He funded this lifestyle by stealing from his respectable customers, taking copies of the keys of cabinets and strongboxes sold in his shop and creeping into their houses to relieve them of their valuables.

Deacon Brodie was caught in the act in 1788 and was hanged in front of a huge crowd. Ironically, he himself had designed improvements to the very gallows used for his execution.

Stevenson took this basic story and transformed it into a chilling examination of human psychology.

Adam Smith and by Dr Samuel Johnson. The court must have been a hotbed of social reform at the time.

At the corner of Lawnmarket and Bank Street is **Deacon Brodie's Tavern**. Named after the city gentleman and infamous burglar, it is one of the best-known pubs in the city. Look left down Bank Street to see the ornate facade of the **Bank of Scotland** headquarters, a symbol of the city's continuing important position in the financial world. The bank was founded in 1695, and is the only body established by the old Scottish Parliament that still exists today. The founding Act is on display, among a wealth of banking paraphernalia, in the **Museum on the Mound** (www.museumonthemound.com; free). For those who can't imagine what a million pounds looks like, one display cabinet contains the sum in (cancelled) banknotes.

The kirk's west window is inspired by Robert Burns

High Street

As you approach St Giles Cathedral, the Royal Mile becomes the **High Street**. On the left you will find a statue of the philosopher and historian David Hume, depicted in a calm, thoughtful pose.

St Giles Cathedral ❻ (officially called the High Kirk of St Giles; www.stgilescathedral.org.uk; free), on your right, was the original parish church for the city and has been at the centre of many of its most important developments. There has been a Christian place of worship on the site since the ninth century. Parts of the interior date back to 1100 and the crown spire is 500 years old; much of the exterior, however, is from the early nineteenth century.

One-hour guided tours of the church take place every day at 10.30am and 2.30pm, but these should be booked in advance. The principal kirk of the Church of Scotland, St Giles was the church of John Knox, the Protestant reformer. From 1559 to 1572 his fiery Calvinist sermons influenced worshippers far beyond the cathedral walls and fuelled the religious discontent that splintered and divided the population.

The small **Thistle Chapel** (built from 1909 to 1911) is dedicated to the Most Ancient and Most Noble Order of the Thistle, the highest order of chivalry in Scotland. The order was founded by James VII (James II of England) and continues today. There are a maximum of sixteen knights at any one time, headed by the reigning monarch. Look up at the pinnacle of each seat and you'll see the carved and painted crests of the present members.

Tours of maximum four visitors can climb the 91 steps to the rooftop for panoramic views and a twenty-minute tour of the clock tower (Sat and Sun; book in advance on the day).

Outside the cathedral in West Parliament Square you will find a statue of John Knox with Bible in hand. It was erected in 1906 not far from the reformer's supposed burial site. Look also for the heart-shaped stone mosaic worked into the cobbles, marking the site of the Edinburgh Tolbooth. The building collected city taxes during the fourteenth century but fulfilled several additional functions in later centuries. It was immortalised in Walter Scott's novel *The Heart of Midlothian* as a prison and place of execution. Passers-by traditionally spit on the cobbled heart to show their contempt.

Parliament Square is also home to **Parliament House**. After its construction in 1639, it held sessions of the Scottish Parliament until

> **NOTES**
>
> To the right of the City Chambers, Anchor Close was once home to the printing works of William Smellie, editor and printer of the first edition of the Encyclopaedia Britannica, which appeared in 1768.

the 'Act of Union' in 1707, but since the nineteenth century it has been an integral part of the Scottish Law Courts. You'll see solicitors walking the alleyways and streets around the building, carrying briefs in hand and garbed in wigs and capes.

Just beyond the east side of the cathedral, topped by a small white unicorn, is the **Mercat Cross**. The first cross erected here, in the fourteenth century, marked the heart of the marketplace and provided a place for royal proclamations to be given a public hearing. It was also a place of execution. The present cross, erected in 1756, is the starting point for many walking tours of the Old Town.

Across High Street you will find Edinburgh's **City Chambers**, housed here since 1811. The building itself was initially constructed to be a royal assembly for merchants, and an area of narrow streets and buildings was covered over and used as foundations. You can descend beneath today's street level and visit one of the 'real' Old Town streets at **The Real Mary King's Close** ❼ (entrance to the left of the City Chambers; www.realmarykingsclose.com; daily; tours released on demand, check online for availability and times). Not for the claustrophobic, this tour is an excellent way of understanding what life was like for those who lived in labyrinth of narrow 'closes' that surrounded both sides of the High Street, where small, tightly packed dwellings saw almost no daylight and living conditions were squalid, cramped and plague-ridden.

Continuing down High Street, you will find **Moubray House** on the left. It is probably the oldest occupied dwelling in Edinburgh, recorded as far back as 1477. Next door is the **Scottish Storytelling Centre** (www.tracscotland.org), a vibrant arts venue that celebrates Scotland's oral traditions, with live storytelling and theatre, and events such as the Scottish International Storytelling Festival in October each year. The centre incorporates a 99-seat auditorium downstairs and **John Knox House ❽**, which dates from 1490. Although it is doubtful the reformer ever lived here, evidence does suggest that he preached from the bow window. Opened as a museum in 1853, the small rooms display Knox memorabilia and the influential manuscripts from which he preached his Calvinist texts.

Directly across High Street from Knox House is the refurbished **Museum of Childhood ❾** (www.edinburghmuseums.org.uk; free). Dedicated to games and toys of yesteryear, you'll find many amusing exhibits of street games, clockwork figures, dolls and teddy bears.

Canongate

The Royal Mile becomes **Canongate** at the point where it intersects St Mary's Street. This is the former boundary of the town of Edinburgh and the neighbouring town, called Canongate, which was a community of aristocrats and members of the royal court serving the Palace of Holyroodhouse. The two towns were united in 1856. Canongate derived its name from an edict by David I (1124–53), founder of the

Museum of Childhood

Abbey of Holyrood, who granted a right to raise a gate between the abbey and the Royal 'burgh' of Edinburgh.

Several historic buildings lead off Canongate, and a number have interesting stories to tell. **Chessel's Court**, on the right, was the place where Deacon Brodie was finally caught in 1788. **Old Playhouse Close** was the site of a theatre where performances resulted in so many riots that it was closed in 1769, after only 20 years. Dating from around 1625, **Moray House** saw a visit from Oliver Cromwell, Lord Protector of England; the house remained in the Moray family until the mid-nineteenth century.

On the left as you walk, you will see the **Canongate Tolbooth** ⓾, with its distinctive clocktower overhanging the pavement. The building on the site dates from 1591 and served as a council chamber and courthouse for the town, in addition to collecting tolls. Today the Tolbooth houses **The People's Story** (www.edinburghmuseums.org.uk; free), a museum charting the history of the ordinary citizens of Edinburgh from the eighteenth century to the present day. Reconstructions of townsfolk at home, at the pub, at high tea or in jail show how people lived in previous eras, augmented by written and oral testimonies.

Facing the Tolbooth is the **Museum of Edinburgh** ⓫ (www.edinburghmuseums.org.uk; free), presenting local-history exhibits from prehistoric times to the present. Huntly House, housing part of the museum, dates from the sixteenth century and contains treasures such as the collar and bowl of 'Greyfriars Bobby' (see page 65). The most exciting venture is 'Foundation – the Story of a City', where Edinburgh literally grows below your feet in a blacked-out theatre.

Nearby **Canongate Kirk** ⓬ was built in 1688, and there are a number of significant figures interred in the peaceful churchyard, including the economist Adam Smith, the poet Robert Fergusson and Mrs Agnes McLehose (the 'Clarinda' of Burns' love poems). Just along from here is **Dunbar's Close Garden**, a pleasant little suntrap.

Across the road and along Crichton's Close you will find the **Scottish Poetry Library** (www.scottishpoetrylibrary.org.uk; free), which gathers a comprehensive collection of contemporary and historic Scottish poetry in a smart modern building. Librarians will help you trace a half-remembered line of Burns or Fergusson.

As you approach the foot of Canongate, nip down **Reid's Close** to get a sneak preview of the Scottish Parliament Building. You'll see the MSP (Member of the Scottish Parliament) block; each member's office has a 'think pod' protruding from the wall. Back on Canongate, as the gates of the Palace of Holyroodhouse come into view, **White Horse Close** can be found on the left. This was the site of the White Horse Inn, the main coaching house at the end of the London–Edinburgh route.

Holyrood

Cross the busy road at the bottom of Canongate to enter the **Holyrood** area, which comprises the palace, abbey and park, along with the Scottish Parliament building. The easternmost stretch of the Royal Mile – only 50 metres/yds long – is called Abbey Strand. It is flanked by a building that protected aristocratic debtors (known as the Abbey Lairds) from arrest and imprisonment; civil authorities had no jurisdiction within the Abbey grounds and could not enter to arrest them.

Canongate Kirk

Palace of Holyroodhouse

The **Palace of Holyroodhouse** ⓭ (www.rct.uk; free audio guide available; closed when royalty is in residence) is the official Scottish home of the reigning British monarch. It began life with a totally different purpose. In 1128 the king, David I, ceded land to the Augustinian order for the creation of the Abbey of Holyrood. He is said to have had a vision of the holy 'rood', or cross, between the antlers of a stag while hunting in this area.

The beautiful abbey was an important centre of worship but continued to have royal connections because of the surrounding hunting grounds. A guesthouse was built adjoining the abbey to be used as a base for royal hunting parties.

Scottish kings came to favour the site, and James IV decided to transform the simple lodgings into a true royal palace. In 1501 he had plans drawn up, which his son James V expanded after his death in 1513. In 1529 work started on a tower and royal apartments for James and his wife, Mary of Guise, which now constitute the western section and tower of the current palace. Mary, Queen of Scots, later occupied apartments here.

Over the next dozen decades, war and fire took their toll, and much rebuilding took place (the great tower, however, survived). Following the return of the British monarchy in 1660, the palace buildings were refurbished and extended. Charles II never saw the palace on which he lavished so much money (the royal coffers expended £57,000, a fortune at the time), but he created the foundation of what we see today, with its amazing ornamental plaster work and carved wood panelling.

NOTES

The Museum of Edinburgh's sign is reference to one of its exhibits – a sedan chair. In the eighteenth century sedan chairs operated in the city much like taxis do today, with licensed sedan carriers transporting the townsfolk.

The Palace of Holyroodhouse

His heir, James VI, lived at the castle in the 1680s, when the paint was barely dry.

During the eighteenth century Holyrood was neglected by succeeding British monarchs, who preferred to stay in their London residence, though Scottish noble families lived within the compound. It was not until 1822, when George IV made a state visit, that the fortunes of the palace revived. Since then, almost every reigning monarch has spent time (or held soirées) at Holyrood, and the palace has been carefully tended throughout the twentieth century. The King usually spends time here in late June and early July.

The **Great Stair** is the formal approach to the royal apartments in the southwestern tower. The plaster ceilings here date from 1678 and depict angels carrying the symbols of royal power: crown, sceptre, sword and wreath of laurel leaves. The **Royal**

Dining Room is situated at the top of the Great Stair. This majestic room is used for modern-day entertaining when the King hosts dinners and banquets. On the walls are portraits of Bonnie Prince Charlie and his brother, Prince Henry.

The **Throne Room** is one of a series of apartments built during the reign of Charles II, though it was originally designed as a guard room that screened entrants to the private chambers beyond. The thrones on view here date from a visit by George V and Queen Mary in 1927.

Two magnificent state rooms follow, both designed by Sir William Bruce as part of the extensions and refurbishment in the 1660s. The **Evening and Morning Drawing Rooms** (originally the Presence Chamber and the Privy Chamber) were designed to meet visiting dignitaries and are splendid in their detail; the oak-panelled ceiling is superbly decorated. Be sure to take a look at the painting above the mantel. The scene, depicting Cupid and Psyche, was considered too risqué for the eyes of Queen Victoria, and during her reign it was covered by a mirror. The **King's Antechamber** was where he entertained his more favoured guests.

The King's Bedchamber is perhaps the most richly decorated room in the royal apartments. Adorning the walls are seventeenth-century tapestries depicting heroic scenes from the life of Alexander the Great. Although the bed dates from the 1680s, it has never been slept in by royalty. It belongs to the Hamilton family, who have served as hereditary keepers of the palace. Beyond is the King's Closet, where only his intimate entourage would be admitted for evenings of drinking and card games.

From the king's apartments you will enter the **Great Gallery**, a long room that is home to 111 portraits of Scottish rulers dating back to antiquity. Commissioned by Charles II, the paintings were all the work of one man, Dutch artist Jacob de Wit. He worked from likenesses of actual monarchs to produce his portraits. For ancient or legendary kings such as Fergus – who was said to have been

Ruins of Holyrood Abbey

related to the Pharaohs of Egypt – fashionable imagery of the time helped to create the finished figures. De Wit was paid a reasonable stipend of £120 per year to produce the works, examples of which can also be seen in other rooms of the palace.

The oldest part of the palace, the **James V Tower** (once called the Great Tower), is for many the highlight of the tour. Its stone walls, which survived both fires in the sixteenth century, sheltered rooms occupied by Mary Stuart and her second husband, Lord Darnley, in the 1560s. On the third floor is the **Bed Chamber of Mary**, **Queen of Scots**, with her antechambers surrounding it. Stairs connect her room to that occupied by her husband.

Nearby is the **Outer Chamber of Mary, Queen of Scots**, where she socialised with her favourites and debated religion with John Knox. It is also where her secretary, David Rizzio, was left to bleed

Arthur's Seat

to death after being stabbed by Lord Darnley and his cronies; a bronze plaque marks the spot. You will find a number of Mary's personal effects on display. The chambers were totally refurbished by Charles II, including larger windows to balance the design of the new extensions. However, the original ceiling of Mary's bedchamber is still in place.

Outside by the entrance, more precious artworks are on view in the King's Gallery. Also set in manicured gardens, are the remains of **Holyrood Abbey**. Today, it comprises little more than the walls of the church nave. The rest of the abbey was razed to the ground in 1570, but the church was saved because it was a parish church and therefore served the local community. Ornate carvings on the stone facade can still just be discerned. A small stone tomb in the southeast corner houses the bones of several members of the royal family. Originally, these all had separate burial sites, but they were sacked by religious protesters. Queen Victoria arranged for the bones of David II, James II, James V and Lord Darnley to be re-interred in a common tomb.

Holyrood Park and Arthur's Seat

To the south of the palace are the green landscapes of **Holyrood Park**, including the volcanic peak known as Arthur's Seat. Once royal hunting grounds, today these areas are used for open-air events and activities. On sunny days this is an ideal family picnic spot. The rugged peak of **Arthur's Seat ⓮**, 823ft (251 metres) in height, can be reached by footpaths all around its base. The path nearest the palace takes walkers along the base of **Salisbury Crags**, a volcanic ridge. The vantage point at the summit of Arthur's Seat offers wonderful views of the city and across the Firth of Forth to the north.

On the far side of Arthur's Seat is **Duddingston Loch**, a bird sanctuary. **Duddingston Kirk**, near the banks of the loch, is one of the oldest Scottish churches still in regular use, founded in the twelfth century. A watchtower was erected in the early 1800s to deter body snatchers. On the causeway leading off Old Church Lane is **Prince Charlie's Cottage**, where the 'Young Pretender' stayed in 1745 while planning his strategy to defeat the English and retake the British throne.

The Scottish Parliament

Back in Holyrood, the **Scottish Parliament Building** ⓯ (www.parliament.scot) is the home of Scotland's devolved democracy. In this

NOTES

The King's Gallery (same opening times as palace, closed Tue & Wed), in front of the palace, features changing exhibits from the priceless royal art collection. Monarchists will adore the shop, which is adjoined by a café.

BUILDING THE SCOTTISH PARLIAMENT

In a referendum of 1997, the Scots voted overwhelmingly for devolution. Donald Dewar, then Scottish Secretary, chose the site of a former brewery for the new parliament and ensured that Catalan architect Enric Miralles won the 1999 competition to design the building. A year later, both Dewer and Miralles had died, leaving the Scottish civil service to grapple with the project's administration, and Miralles' architectural firm to puzzle over his sketches.

Six years and a budget-busting £500 million later, the building was finished. Some love it, some hate it. What is largely agreed is that the interior of the building far outstrips the exterior. Despite the considerable use of concrete and granite, Miralles intended the parliament complex to resemble a plant. Each of the seven buildings forms a leaf of the plant, connected at the centre by the Garden Lobby. Leaf-shaped skylights allow daylight to illuminate the activity of the MSPs in the lobby, who pause here for a drink or to be interviewed by journalists at the foot of the staircase leading to the Debating Chamber. Be sure to visit the chamber, whether or not a debate is in session. The ceiling is a marvel – roof beams are held up by 112 steel nodes, all of different sizes. Look out too for bottle-shaped cut-outs on the west wall – symbolising not whisky bottles, rather the people of Scotland looking in on the work of Parliament.

Despite the Scottish Parliament Building's controversial aspects, it is remarkably accessible to the visiting public. And even on a gloomy day the building is infused with light, accentuating the feeling of open government.

sprawling complex of seven buildings, Members of the Scottish Parliament (or MSPs) question the First Minister and his/her cabinet, and legislate on health, education and other domestic matters. If you wish to see Parliament at work, visit on a business day and attend a Committee meeting or a parliamentary debate (ticket required; free). Visitors are welcome to explore all public areas without booking a tour.

Directly in front of Parliament, on Holyrood Road, is **Dynamic Earth** 16 (www.dynamicearth.co.uk), a futuristic building under a brilliant white-tented roof. This is an interactive journey through the history of the Earth from the moment of the 'Big Bang'. Using the latest technology, the exhibits are entertaining and educational for all ages, posing questions about our roles as managers of the Earth's resources and the planet's future. The fun parts include getting to touch an iceberg, experiencing the effects of a bubbling volcano and witnessing a crash landing in the rainforest. The tour de force is the 3D cinema that delivers amazing 4D effects that allow you to touch, feel and smell the experience as you journey across the globe; it even snows on the audience.

The Debating Chamber is at the heart of Parliament

Grassmarket and Greyfriars

In the shadows of the southern walls of Edinburgh Castle lies the rectangular space of **Grassmarket**. From 1477 this was a marketplace for local farmers as well as one of the main sites for executions. Huge crowds would gather for the gory events – as they did for the markets – and a series of hostelries and pubs set up business to cater for them. Some still operate, putting out tables in summer so you can enjoy alfresco food and drinks. At the eastern end of Grassmarket there is a memorial to the Covenanters (Scottish Protestant clergymen) martyred by Catholic Stuart kings in the seventeenth century.

From Grassmarket, **Cowgate** runs parallel to the Royal Mile to Holyrood on a lower level. The road has a number of bridges spanning its route, creating a shadowy, dark and almost sombre appearance. The alleyways and passages leading off this thoroughfare are some of the oldest in the city. Sadly, a fire destroyed a large chunk of the central passage in 2002.

Cowgate was known for generations as the Irish Quarter because many families came here to escape the potato famine in their own country. At the western end (where Cowgate meets Holyrood Road), you will see one of the few remaining sections of

Outdoor drinking and markets in Grassmarket

GREYFRIARS BOBBY

One of the most famous inhabitants of Edinburgh, Greyfriars Bobby was a Skye terrier belonging to 'Auld Jock' Gray, a local police constable. When Jock died in 1858, Bobby followed the funeral procession to the graveyard at Greyfriars Church and then stayed at his master's grave for the next fourteen years, leaving it only to look for food at the nearby tavern.

Though he was legally a stray and thus under threat of being destroyed, the whole city rallied around the faithful dog. The Lord Provost issued a licence that allowed Bobby to maintain his vigil, which he did until his death in 1873. He was buried in the graveyard, and a statue, financed by public donations, was erected outside the tavern. Bobby's collar and bowl can be seen at the Museum of Edinburgh, and his story has been told in a Walt Disney movie and a feature film starring Christopher Lee.

the **Flodden Wall**, which was begun after the Scottish defeat at the Battle of Flodden in 1513.

West Bow and **Candlemaker Row** are streets leading away from Cowgate Head and the east end of Grassmarket. Here you'll find interesting shops for antiques, collectibles, comestibles and antiquarian books. Both these streets lead to the upper level of the George IV Bridge.

From Candlemaker Row, enter the Greyfriars Churchyard through a gate on the right. The **Greyfriars Church** ⓱ was closely linked with the Protestant Covenanters, and many of those hanged in the Grassmarket are buried here. The church was opened in 1620, and the National Covenant was signed here in 1638. The church became a barracks during Oliver Cromwell's occupation of the city in the 1650s; in 1718 there was an explosion of gunpowder that had been stored in the tower. Fire wreaked further damage in 1845. Greyfriars Church was restored in 1938 to produce the building you see now.

The **graveyard** has some ornate tombs, with skulls, crossbones and other symbols of death. Gravestones rest along the tenement walls marking the outer perimeter. Among those buried here are George Buchanan, tutor to Mary, Queen of Scots; James Craig, architect of Edinburgh's New Town; and Joseph Black, physicist and chemist. Just beside the main entrance is the grave of Greyfriars Bobby. From here you can see some of the best views of the layout of the Old Town, with layer upon layer of crenulated rooftops and hundreds of chimney stacks.

The main gate of the churchyard leads out to Greyfriars Place, and across the street you will find an excellent view of the **National Museum of Scotland** ⓲ (www.nms.ac.uk; free). With its main entrance on Chambers Street, the museum is housed in a remarkable building designed by architects Benson and Forsyth. It charts the history of Scotland, bringing under one roof a number of important collections of artefacts. The story begins 3.4 billion years ago with displays of fossils and rock, marking the geological changes that forged the landscape. It continues through the turbulent eras of Scottish history, and on to the industrial developments of modern times.

The main hall of the Grand Gallery, augmented by its towering pillars, would provide an impressive place to start any museum visit. Light pours through the high windows, enhancing the objects on display in this extraordinary collection. Of particular note here is the Millennium clock that, every hour on the hour, delights with its music and light performance as the figures comes to life.

Look through the arch at the eastern end of the Grand Gallery and you'll see a Tyrannosaurus rex guarding a stunning series of galleries about the Natural World. Beyond here, various other exhibition spaces allow you to travel through the country's history, explore ideas and inventions from some of Scotland's finest innovators and gain an insight into world cultures. Ten innovative galleries showcase the collections of decorative art, design, fashion, science and technology.

Other facilities include three shops, the informal *Balcony Café*, which offers freshly prepared food with great views over the Grand Gallery, and the *Museum Brasserie* (see page 117).

The National Museum of Scotland is at the heart of the old **University of Edinburgh** quarter, whose students still attend lectures in the nearby sandstone buildings. The university's Old College building holds the **Talbot Rice Gallery** ⓳ (www.ed.ac.uk/talbot-rice; free). Here, contemporary visual art is displayed in the White Gallery, while the Georgian Gallery, designed by William Playfair, exhibits the university's collection of Old Master paintings, sculptures and Renaissance bronzes.

The city has a reputation for research and development in medicine, which began in 1505 with the founding of, what would become, the Royal College of Surgeons, followed by the Royal College of Physicians in 1681 and the School of Medicine a few years later. You can probe further into the city's medical history at the **Surgeons' Hall Museums** ⓴ (www.museum.rcsed.ac.uk) on Nicolson Street. The museum's newest permanent gallery, the 2022-opened Body Voyager, takes visitors on a journey through the human body, exploring how technology is changing the course of surgery and patient care.

Scottish National Gallery

NOTES

As the New Town was established at the close of the eighteenth century, the city's social divisions were, for the first time, reflected in its geography. The 'Great Flitting' saw the well-off haul their belongings across the Mound to the spacious new suburb, leaving the poor to live in cramped slum conditions.

Also on Nicolson Street is the **Edinburgh Festival Theatre** (see page 95).

Although the university campus has mushroomed, with sites across the city, the streets here have inexpensive eateries, with an eclectic range of shops selling clothes, music and books.

South of the museums, a short walk down Forest Road and with its entrance on Lauriston Place, stands the ornate **George Heriot's School**. Although not open to the public, its towers and beautifully carved stone walls can be seen from vantage points across the city. 'Jinglin' Geordie' Heriot was a banker, goldsmith and jeweller to James IV. When he died in 1624, his fortune was bequeathed to the education and upkeep of orphans, and the school was built to this end.

The New Town

Highlights

- **Princes Street**, see page 71
- **George Street**, see page 75
- **National Galleries of Scotland: National**, see page 72
- **National Galleries of Scotland: Portrait**, see page 78
- **Calton Hill**, see page 79

By the beginning of the eighteenth century, life in the city of Edinburgh (today's Old Town) was overcrowded and unsanitary. The city had grown very little since the fourteenth century, yet its population was said to be over 50,000. Large families lived in high tenements, sharing a well with hundreds of other families. Sewage and dirty water were thrown from upper floors to the streets below and left to fester.

In 1725 the Lord Provost of the city, George Drummond, first raised the possibility of expansion to the northeast, across what was called Barefoot's Parks to the green fields beyond. His ideas were not made official until 1752, and it was another fourteen years before plans were put into place for a competition to create a design for this new development, to be called the **New Town**.

There were logistical problems to be overcome. At the foot of the castle was Nor' Loch, a large expanse of water that required draining. There would also have to be adequate access between

View across the New Town

NOTES

Today, the streets of the New Town have perhaps the greatest collection of Georgian architecture in the world. Together with the Old Town, the New Town is a UNESCO World Heritage Site, safeguarding its special character.

the older and newer parts of town, including a bridge over the valley between Barefoot's Parks and the Royal Mile.

The competition winner, announced in 1766, was James Craig, an unknown 23-year-old architect and native of the city. His plan was a simple grid: a symmetrical design with straight streets and grand squares. The recent union with England was the inspiration for street names such as 'Rose' and 'Thistle'. The royal family was honoured with George Street, Queen Street and Princes Street. Surprisingly, the plan contained little detail for the buildings to line the streets and frame the squares. Instead, Craig concentrated on the overall design.

In 1763 construction had already begun on North Bridge, which would provide access from the Old Town. Nor' Loch was drained (creating land for today's Princes Street Gardens), and the Mound was constructed to provide a second, westerly access between the two settlements.

The first houses built here did not adhere to any set design. In 1782, after only a few years, the city decided to impose planning guidelines. At the same time, an architect named Robert Adam became popular in the fashionable circles of the well-to-do, having made a name for himself in England. It was he who would add the 'flesh' of handsome buildings to the 'bones' of Craig's design.

By the beginning of the nineteenth century, the New Town had become so popular that plans were made for a second stage. This would be a largely residential area extending north from Queen Street, incorporating a number of roundabouts (circuses) as well as straight roads. Most influential at this stage was architect William

Playfair, and his flair can be seen in many of the streets and public buildings of the time. These streets are still largely residential and make an interesting area to explore, displaying an abundance of original detail. Edinburgh became known as the 'Athens of the North' for both its aesthetic beauty and its wealth of talented artists, philosophers and scientists. Because so many buildings are still used as residences, there are relatively few attractions to visit compared with the Old Town.

Princes Street

Looking north from the high ground of the Old Town, the first street you can see is **Princes Street**. It was once regarded as the most beautiful street in Europe, a claim that is difficult to appreciate today since so many of the original buildings have been replaced. There are splendid views of the castle all along its length.

Princes Street

On the south side of the street – in the open ground below the castle and on the site of the formerly marshy Nor' Loch – are **Princes Street Gardens**, a welcome place to relax on a sunny day. The West Gardens have a number of interesting memorial statues and sculptures, including the **Scottish American War Memorial** (World War I) and the **Royal Scots Memorial**.

At the centre of the gardens is the **Ross Open Air Theatre** (for show times tel: 0131 228 1155), which plays host to free concerts throughout the year, particularly during the festival season. During the summer, beside the flight of steps carrying people up to the Mound, you will find the **Floral Clock** ㉑. Planted with hundreds of pretty blooms, all in pristine condition, it has kept accurate time since its creation in 1903.

The West and East Gardens are split by the **Mound**, an artificial slope of rock and soil that carries a road connecting the New Town with the Old. Set back from Princes Street is the **National Galleries of Scotland: National** ㉒ (www.nationalgalleries.org; free), opened in 1859, which houses works by native Scottish artists and international masters in one of two grand Neoclassical buildings at the foot of the Mound (the other shows temporary exhibitions organised by the National Galleries of Scotland and the Royal Scottish Academy of Art and Architecture).

The collection – and indeed the building itself – is not as vast as national collections found elsewhere, but the National does boast a world-class curation, ranging from Renaissance and early modern artworks to some superb Impressionist and Post-Impressionist works, and of course, the very best Scottish art.

Raphael's *Bridgewater Madonna*, Velázquez's *An Old Woman Cooking Eggs* and Sir Edwin Landseer's famous *Monarch of the Glen* are only three from a collection that includes pieces by Titian, Rubens, Constable, Turner, Monet and Van Gogh. Scottish artists include Allan Ramsay, Sir Henry Raeburn and Sir David Wilkie. Among the National's most valuable treasures is **Hugo van der Goes**' *Trinity Altarpiece*, on long-term loan from the King. Painted in the mid-fifteenth century, the paintings were commissioned by Provost Edward Bonkil for the Holy Trinity Collegiate Church, which was later demolished to make way for Edinburgh's Waverley Station. Bonkil can be seen amid the company of organ-playing angels in the finest and best-preserved of the four panels, while on the reverse sides are portraits of James III, his son (the future James IV) and Queen Margrethe of Denmark.

The £30-million **Weston Link** is a huge underground passage that burrows through the Mound and connects the Scottish National Gallery with the Royal Scottish Academy. Visitor facilities here include a 200-seat lecture theatre (free lunchtime lectures are given by gallery experts), touch-screen displays to explore the collections and a garden-side café and restaurant.

Designed almost as the Scottish National Gallery's twin, the **Royal Scottish Academy** ㉓ holds regular exhibitions of Scottish and international art, as well as displays by its members.

Between the two buildings, **East Princes Gardens** are smaller than the West Gardens. As part of the Hogmanay celebrations an ice rink covers the lawns, where you can enjoy outdoor skating in a picturesque setting for a few weeks. Rising above the flower beds is the solemn **Scott Monument** ㉔ (www.edinburghmuseums.org.uk), a huge, stone neo-Gothic structure with four buttresses supporting a spire. The whole edifice is 200ft (61 metres) high. Within sits the statue of novelist Sir Walter Scott (and his faithful dog, Maida) carved from Cararra marble. Designed

The castle viewed from Princes Street Gardens

The Scott Monument

by George Meikle Kemp, a self-taught draughtsman of humble birth, the monument took its inspiration from the design of Melrose Abbey, which lies south of Edinburgh in the Borders. Carved into the structure are 64 statuettes representing characters from Scott's books. Steps (287 in all) inside the outer columns lead up to galleries spread across four levels.

The **view** from the topmost gallery is spectacular.

Beyond the monument is Waverley Bridge. Here you can board buses for a tour of city attractions. This is also the site of **Waverley Station**, and the sound of arriving trains can be heard as background noise throughout the day. The lines take a dramatic route via ditches cut through Princes Street Gardens and under the Mound (in the National Gallery you can feel a faint movement as the trains travel underneath).

On the south side of the station is Market Street, which was one of the principal market sites during the Victorian era. Market Street is home to the **Edinburgh City Art Centre** (www.edinburghmuseums.org.uk; free), showcasing nationally recognised Scottish art alongside the work of up-and-coming artists over six floors of an impressive former warehouse.

At the eastern end of Princes Street is **General Register House**, completed in 1788 from a design by Robert Adam. As part of the **National Records of Scotland** (www.nrscotland.gov.uk), it stashes historical records, such as those created by Scottish government, businesses, landed estates, families, courts and churches. Behind is **New Register House**, which stores records of births, marriages and deaths in Scotland, while in front is a statue of the Duke of Wellington, resplendent in battle dress astride his steed, Copenhagen.

George Street

The centrepiece of Craig's original design for the New Town was **George Street**. The grand thoroughfare, anchored at each end by a large square, had a symmetrical pattern of streets on both its flanks. George Street was the traditional centre of Edinburgh's financial district, where many successful bankers increased the wealth of their trusting investors. Scottish banking has long been held in high regard and still plays an important part in the financial world. However, the buildings – beautiful though they are – have not been able to accommodate modern computerised banking equipment; and many institutions have moved to modern

SECRET GARDENS

Like many cities, Edinburgh has picturesque gardens among its paved streets and rows of houses. Unlike most other cities, however, many of these gardens are private and enjoyed by only a favoured few.

When the New Town was planned in the 1760s, it incorporated squares (such as St Andrew) and green spaces (such as Queen Street Gardens) as an integral part of the design. The gardens were held in common by the householders who lived around them, with each household having a key to gain access through locked, wrought-iron gates.

The rights and responsibilities of the 'keyholders' have been passed down through the generations, and today these gates are still locked to the general public. The fine statues and manicured lawns may be viewed from the outside only.

NOTES

The Scots have always been among the modern world's most successful bankers, and Edinburgh is one of Europe's biggest financial centres. Unlike their English counterparts, three Scottish clearing banks retain the right to print their own distinctive banknotes.

premises around the city. This hasn't made George Street an empty shell. Where the banks have cleared out, fashionable shops, bars and restaurants have moved in.

The western end of George Street begins at **Charlotte Square** ㉕, originally named St George's Square after England's patron saint (mirroring St Andrew Square at the street's eastern end). The name was changed to honour Queen Charlotte – George III's wife – who felt a little upset at having been left out of the original plans. After all, her husband and two sons had roads named after them: George Street and Princes Street.

Charlotte Square is arguably the jewel of the New Town. The facades of elegant houses on the north side were designed by Robert Adam and have changed little since they were finished in 1805. In the centre of the terrace is **Georgian House**, owned by the National Trust for Scotland and restored in period style to show the workings of a typical Georgian household; even the floorboards have been dry scrubbed in the original manner. All of the many items in the house are authentic, including a huge array of kitchen utensils, furniture, carpets and curtains. Curiously, the bedchamber is on the ground floor; upper-floor bedrooms became fashionable at a later date. The basement kitchen is a masterpiece of late eighteenth-century domestic technology.

On the western flank of the square, **West Register House**, designed originally by Robert Reid in 1811 as a church (St George's), was taken over by the government in 1960 and is now part of the **National Records of Scotland**. The building at the corner of

Charlotte Square and South Charlotte Street was the birthplace of Alexander Graham Bell, inventor of the telephone.

Heading east along George Street you will pass the nineteenth-century **Assembly Rooms** (www.assemblyroomsedinburgh.co.uk). With their magnificent chandeliers, the rooms have been the setting for many great social occasions and are used as a venue for stage performances. Across the road is the **Church of St Andrew and St George** ㉖ (1785), whose oval-shaped interior witnessed the 'Great Disruption' of 1843. At the far end of George Street, the most stunning building on **St Andrew Square** is that belonging to the **Royal Bank of Scotland**. Originally a house, it was designed by Sir William Chambers and completed in 1772; the dome was added in 1858.

Scottish National Portrait Gallery

National Galleries of Scotland: Portrait

From St Andrew Square it is only a short walk north to Queen Street, where you will find the **National Galleries of Scotland: Portrait** ㉗ (www.nationalgalleries.org; free) on the corner. More than two hundred paintings of famous – and infamous – Scots are spread across fourteen galleries. The collection was initiated by David, eleventh Earl of Buchan. Following the earl's death, Scottish historian Thomas Carlyle decided to inspire his fellow countrymen through a national gallery devoted to their heroes. He obtained private backing for the creation of the gallery, which opened in 1889.

Designed by Sir Robert Rowand Anderson, the red-sandstone Gothic Revival palace is encrusted with statues depicting Scottish poets, artists and dignitaries. The two-storey entrance (Great Hall) features William Hole's beautifully detailed frieze just below the cornice. The Great Hall is also home to several sculptures, including one of Carlyle, the gallery's founding father.

A glass lift ascends to fourteen carefully restored galleries, flooded in natural light and filled with an ever-rotatory roster of exhibits that bring to life some of the great individuals who have made their mark on Scottish history, from Mary, Queen of Scots and Robert Burns to more recent legends in sport and the arts, such as Manchester United's manager Sir Alex Ferguson and actor Ncuti Gatwa. Thematic short-term exhibitions have included ARTIST ROOMS Self Evidence, which celebrated the work of three of the twentieth century's most-influential photographers: Francesca Woodman, Diane Arbus and Robert Mapplethorpe; and Before and After Coal, which explored the history and legacy of coal through photographs and voices of Scottish mining communities.

The Library and Print Room (visit by appointment only) houses over 50,000 works of art on paper, including the interesting Photography Collection, and is also home to a notable collection of portrait miniatures.

Calton Hill

From the eastern end of Princes Street, the eye is drawn to a hill topped with a series of intriguing, disparate buildings. This is **Calton Hill** ㉘, built around 328ft (100 metres) of hard volcanic rock. Its monuments and architecture are said to have been another contributor to Edinburgh's epithet 'Athens of the North'. You will be met by a flight of steep steps, but the superb views across the city make the climb worthwhile.

At the hill's crest, you will find the **City Observatory**, which for many years stood as an abandoned ruin. However, arts organisation Collective (www.collective-edinburgh.art) has now given the buildings a new lease of life, restoring and transforming them – alongside a new purpose-built exhibition space – into a spectacular gallery. The Old Observatory here is the only building designed by James Craig left in the city (completed in 1792). Playfair's New Observatory was built in 1818 and granted Royal Observatory status in 1822, although the smoky skies and train steam over the city made it an unsuitable location for watching the stars. The Royal Observatory was eventually relocated to Blackford Hill, further south, in 1895.

The nearby **Nelson Monument** (www.edinburghmuseums.org.uk), an elegant

National Monument, Calton Hill

Dean Village and the Water of Leith

tower 98ft (30 metres) high, commemorates the naval victory at Trafalgar in 1805. You can climb the column for incredible panoramic views of the city and the Firth of Forth to the north. Make sure to bring your camera with you here. At the top of the tower is a white ball on a metal stake. As one o'clock approaches, the ball rises to the top of the stake and then drops exactly on the stroke of one. This device is a visual counterpart to the firing of the One O'Clock Gun at the Castle. It could easily be seen by ships in the Firth of Forth and was a useful safeguard if prevailing winds carried the sound of the gunfire the wrong way.

A colonnaded circular monument to the right was raised in the memory of Dugald Stewart, professor of moral philosophy at the University of Edinburgh in the 1780s. The classical design was taken from examples in Athens.

The most fascinating structure on Calton Hill is the **National Monument**. What looks from a distance like a huge Greek temple with many Doric columns turns out to be only a single facade with twelve columns. It was planned in the 1820s as a symbol of Scottish national pride and designed as a mini-Parthenon, in deference to the Neoclassical style popular at the time. Unfortunately, the public was not enthusiastic, the funding ran out and the project was abandoned, giving the monument its other name: 'Scotland's Disgrace'.

Edinburgh's villages

Highlights

- **Dean Village**, see page 81
- **National Galleries of Scotland: Modern**, see page 82
- **Inverleith**, see page 84
- **Corstorphine**, see page 85
- **Leith**, see page 86
- **Cramond**, see page 88

Edinburgh has throughout most of its history been a very compact city. Even the New Town had very set boundaries. The entire city was surrounded by open countryside with a scattering of small villages. But massive growth during the twentieth century saw Edinburgh absorb many of these formerly independent communities into its ever-enlarging limits. Surprisingly – and happily – the villages did not allow their character to be diluted and swallowed up into one homogenous suburb. They still maintain their own individual charms and are an important element in Edinburgh's continuing appeal.

Dean Village

Less than half a mile (0.8km) from the western end of Princes Street is **Dean Village** ㉙, which straddles the ribbon-thin Water of Leith, whose narrow valley drops steeply here. Dean Bridge carries the main road over the Water; it was designed and built by Thomas Telford, one of Scotland's greatest civil engineers.

Dean was an industrial village, its economy depending on numerous small mills that have now completely disappeared. A walk beside the water offers the most interesting views, so don't cross the bridge. Instead, take the cobbled alley of Bells Brae to Hawthornbank Road down into the valley. You'll find great views of the rear of the Georgian houses of the New Town as well as the small cottages of Dean Village itself.

A ten-minute walk east on Belford Road brings you to the **National Galleries of Scotland: Modern** 30 (www.nationalgalleries.org; free), founded in 1959. Scotland's national collection of modern and contemporary art is housed in two Neoclassical buildings, Modern One and Modern Two, set in parkland dotted with sculptures by important artists like Richard Long, Henry Moore, Rachel Whiteread and, most strikingly, Charles Jencks, whose prize-winning *Landform*, a swirling mix of ponds and grassy mounds, dominates the area in front of the gallery entrance.

The art collection here has a strong Scottish contingent, with a particularly fine body of works from the early twentieth-century Colourists, such as Samuel Peploe, John Duncan Fergusson and Leslie Hunter. Scots-born painters who spent enough time in France to blend post-Impressionist ideas with Scottish painting traditions, these leading figures of the movement are known for their fluid paint handling and use of vivid colours. International works from the same period feature crowd-pleasers like Matisse and Picasso, alongside a world-class collection of Surrealism featuring work by Magritte, Dalí, Carrington and Varo, and a solid postwar catalogue with pieces by Hockney, Warhol and Kusama.

The gallery has also picked up a considerable curation of contemporary material from living British exponents of modern art such as Damien Hirst and Tracey Emin. **Modern One** draws on the gallery's enviable collection to bolster the temporary exhibitions on show. The building is divided into 22 exhibition spaces spread over two floors, with a good mix of audiovisual and sculpture complementing the main display, while a ground-floor café with outdoor terrace sits alongside a well-stocked book and gift shop.

Occupying a fine Victorian mansion across the road, **Modern Two** 31 was dramatically refurbished to make space for the work of Edinburgh-born sculptor Sir Eduardo Paolozzi, described by some as the father of Pop Art. On permanent display is his huge sculpture, *Vulcan*, a half-man, half-machine squeezed into the Great Hall – view it both from ground level and the head-height balcony to appreciate its sheer scale. To the right of the main entrance, a room has been expertly reimagined as Paolozzi's studio, down to the clutter

National Galleries of Scotland: Modern

of half-finished casts, toys and empty pots of glue. The remaining rooms are normally given over to temporary exhibitions.

Inverleith

Immediately north of Edinburgh's New Town is **Inverleith**, an area full of green sites. Large schools with acres of grounds, playing fields and recreation areas are interspersed with sumptuous houses set in leafy lanes. It was here that the **Royal Botanic Garden** 32 (www.rbge.org.uk; free, charge for glasshouse) was moved in 1823 from a location not far from the Abbey of Holyrood. The garden had been founded as early as 1670 as a resource for medical research, affiliated for many years with the Royal College of Physicians.

Monkey puzzle tree in the Royal Botanic Garden

The present site covers 70 acres (28 hectares) of ground divided into several different natural environments. The huge Victorian glasshouse, the Temperate Palm House, is impressive and packed with ferns and palms that thrive in the warm, damp environment. A large 1960s glasshouse sits beside it and, though lacking the elegance of its neighbour, still boasts an impressive collection. The surrounding landscaped grounds are kept in pristine condition. Mature trees shade lawns and flower beds that are home to numerous bird species and cheeky grey squirrels. You can also wander through the soothing Chinese garden, with its waterfalls and pretty red pergola. Note: all the glasshouses will be closed until at least 2027 while a major restoration project takes place.

The Signal Tower, Leith

Corstorphine

About three miles (5km) west of Edinburgh's centre, past the rugby ground at Murrayfield, you will find **Corstorphine**. For centuries this was a farming village, separated from the city by the green expanse of Corstorphine Hill. **Edinburgh Zoo** ㉝ (www.edinburghzoo.org.uk) is spread out across the hillside with visitors needing to climb some inclines to the upper enclosures.

The zoo opened in 1913 and was designed with enclosures rather than cages, a new idea at the time. This offered a more natural habitat for animals and a clearer view for visitors. When the zoo celebrated the first successful hatching in captivity of a king penguin in 1919, it gained world renown: no other zoo had examples of this penguin species. In fact, the zoo boasts the world's only knighted penguin – Brigadier Sir Nils Olav. Today, the zoo continues work on the conservation of animal species and acts as an educational resource. There are over 127 species on view here, including endangered rhinos and chimpanzees, beautiful big cats and herds of zebra. The zoo's hitherto most famous residents – giant pandas Tian Tian and Yang Guang – were returned to China in 2023, though there are still plenty of highlights, not least the Wee Waddle (penguin parade Thurs–Sun 2.15pm) and the Budongo Trail – a chimpanzee enclosure with intimate viewing positions.

Leith

Situated on the coast, **Leith** ㉞ is three miles (5km) from the city centre. It has been an important settlement since the fourteenth century and was the largest port in Scotland for many years, handling Edinburgh's cargo. It was a fiercely independent settlement with its own fishing fleet and shipbuilding industry. In 1920 Leith was incorporated into the city of Edinburgh.

Royal Yacht Britannia

After a brief twentieth-century decline, Leith's fortunes have revived. The old warehouses have been transformed into upmarket apartments and fashionable office buildings, and there is a buzz of chic commercial activity that has spawned smart restaurants and bars. Local authorities have restored some of Leith's handsome commercial buildings, such as the grand **Custom House**, the **Corn Exchange** and **Leith Assembly Rooms**. Older locals – trawler men or dockworkers – might lament the loss of Leith's gritty, salt-of-the-earth reputation, but the town has an air of excitement about it. Buses and a 2023-revitalised tram from the city centre will carry you here in minutes.

Situated in the **Ocean Terminal** leisure and shopping complex (designed by Sir Terence Conran) is the **Royal Yacht *Britannia*** 35 (www.royalyachtbritannia.co.uk; booking advisable). Decommissioned in 1997, the yacht once transported Elizabeth II and her official representatives on 968 royal and diplomatic visits to venues around the world.

The 412ft (125-metre) three-masted ship was launched in April 1953, when Elizabeth II was in the first few months of her reign. *Britannia* travelled all over the world, entertaining princes, presidents and diplomats. But she is perhaps best remembered as the royal honeymoon boat. Princess Margaret began the tradition, to be followed by three of the Queen Elizabeth II's children: Anne, Andrew and Charles, who journeyed with the newly designated Diana, Princess of Wales, around the Mediterranean in 1981. A visitor centre introduces the yacht, its crew and the royal patrons, and on board you can see the royal apartments (designed by Sir Hugh Casson in the style of an English country house), grand dining room, Admiral's quarters and engine room.

The most attractive part of Leith is the **Shore**, a short walk east of *Britannia*. The Shore formed around the mouth of the Water of Leith, the narrow river running through Edinburgh. Even here the Water is really little more than a large stream, but it flows into the Firth of Forth and beyond into the North Sea. Downstream, the river's final twist opens wide as the boats and restaurants of Leith's harbour come into view.

The Shore comprises a quayside and knot of cobbled lanes sheltering three of Edinburgh's seven Michelin-starred restaurants, quaint traditional pubs, cafés and bars; it's the ideal finishing point for a walk along the river.

A little way to the south are **Leith Links**, said to be the birthplace of golf, where the Honourable Company of Edinburgh

The Forth Bridge

Golfers built a clubhouse in 1767, now a public park with tree-lined walkways and a venue for the Edinburgh Mela Festival).

Cramond

At present-day **Cramond** ㊱, located at the mouth of the River Almond, the Romans constructed a fort in the second century AD at the eastern end of their defensive Antonine Wall. The foundations of the fort can still be seen, and artefacts from the site are displayed in the Museum of Edinburgh (see page 54). Sailing boats dock at Cramond, where the tidal river spills into the Firth of Forth. Much of the village is from the eighteenth century, and the whitewashed cottages are very picturesque. There are pleasant walks along the coastline to the Cramond Inn (closed until further notice), believed to be a setting described in Stevenson's *St Ives*.

Excursions

Highlights

- **South Queensferry and the Forth bridges**, see page 89
- **Hopetoun House and Linlithgow Palace**, see page 90
- **East Lothian**, see page 91
- **Rosslyn Chapel**, see page 91

An effortless day's outing from the capital brings you within reach of much of Scotland's past and present and the forces that have shaped the country: its critical topography, its dominant families and its gifted architects.

South Queensferry and the Forth bridges

Approximately eight miles (13km) west of the city is **South Queensferry** ❸❼, a town that developed as a crossing point of the Forth for routes to the north of Scotland. It is said that Queen Margaret, later St Margaret, often travelled this route in the late eleventh century and that the town took its name from her journeys. A plaque on the water's edge at the Binks (a natural jetty formed by a rocky outcrop) marks her landing site.

The Victorian solution for crossing the Forth resulted in one of the greatest engineering achievements of the era, the **Forth Bridge**. Completed in 1890, the bridge comprises three huge cantilevers joined by two suspended spans, for a total length of 4746ft (1447 metres). For many years it was the longest bridge in the world, overshadowing the town which sits on the banks of the river below. Maintenance is a mammoth task, and painters work constantly on the structure.

In 1964 a sister structure, the **Forth Road Bridge**, was completed to take vehicular traffic across the Firth. The bridge is a single, unsupported span 3300ft (1006 metres) in length. Completing this iconic trio is the **Queensferry Crossing**, the UK's longest road bridge, provides a major upgrade to the way traffic crosses the Forth. From a small jetty below the railway bridge, you can take a ferry out into the Firth of Forth to tiny **Inchcolm Island** 38 (www.maidoftheforth.co.uk; sailings most days June–Aug, less frequent April–May and Sept–Oct). Here lies the ruined Abbey of St Colm, founded in the twelfth century and named after St Columba, who had brought Christianity to western Scotland six hundred years earlier.

Hopetoun House and Linlithgow Palace

Situated twelve miles (19km) to the west of Edinburgh is **Hopetoun House** 39 (www.hopetoun.co.uk), the historic family home of the earls and marquesses of Linlithgow. Begun in 1699 by William Bruce, William Adam completed the building. Most of the original eighteenth-century furniture and wall coverings can still be seen, as well as opulent gilding and fine classical motifs. The house is set in 150 acres (60 hectares) of parkland. The rooftop offers great views of the Forth bridges.

Rosslyn Chapel

Linlithgow itself, a few miles further west, is home to the ruins of **Linlithgow Palace** 40 (www.historicenvironment.scot/visit-a-place). Built by James I in 1425, the palace witnessed key events in Scottish history. In 1513 Queen Margaret waited here for the return of her husband James IV, unaware of his death at the hands of the English in the Battle of Flodden. In 1542 Mary, Queen of Scots, was born here, and the future Charles I was raised at the palace. Oliver Cromwell wintered at Linlithgow during his 1650 punitive trip to Scotland. A century later the palace was gutted by fire following Bonnie Prince Charlie's retreat from England. The extensive remains give an impressive idea of the scale and splendour of the palace in its heyday.

East Lothian

East of Edinburgh is the benign and affluent terrain of **East Lothian**. Its rolling farmland is ornamented with pretty, coastal villages and the northern coastline is dotted with bays, beaches and bird-haunted islands. The sandy links give it some of the best golf courses in the world.

Visit **Portobello** to savour the faded charm of a delightful, old-fashioned seaside resort. Prosperous Victorian families from Edinburgh spent summers here on the wide sandy beach. Handsome Georgian terraces testify to the town's wealthy past.

Rosslyn Chapel

Southwest of the city lies the former mining village of Roslin and, beyond, the beautiful woodlands of **Roslin Glen Country Park**, which provide the backdrop to **Rosslyn Castle**, constructed by Henry Sinclair, Earl of Orkney, during the fourteenth century. The Sinclair family are buried in the small **Rosslyn Chapel** ❹❶ (www.rosslynchapel.com), which is elaborately decorated inside with carvings of the Seven Cardinal Virtues and Seven Deadly Sins. Look out for the beautiful **Apprentice Pillar**.

The chapel became famous following the huge success of *The Da Vinci Code* by Dan Brown. In the novel it is claimed that the Holy Grail was once hidden at Rosslyn and that the descendants of Jesus and Mary Magdalene can be traced to the chapel.

A walk up Arthur's Seat will be rewarded with fantastic views

Things to do

Though it is Edinburgh's history that looms large in its volcano-crowned castle and imposing Royal Mile, on the ground unfolds a rich cultural sphere, independent music scene and one of the best festival calendars in the world.

Festivals

Edinburgh's streets burst into life in July and August when a number of separate festivals and events run concurrently. The city almost comes apart at the seams, with visitors jostling for street space with performers, clowns, face painters and numerous small crafts markets.

For more information, you can access websites for all the festivals at www.edinburghfestivalcity.com (for ticket and contact information, see page 139).

Edinburgh International Festival

In the wake of World War II, Edinburgh's Lord Provost, Sir John Falconer, envisaged a great celebration of the arts, which would bring nations closer together and re-establish Edinburgh as a European city of culture on a worldwide stage. In 1947 Edinburgh hosted its first International Festival and, with opera impresario Rudolf Bing at the helm, it was a great success, rapidly becoming one of the foremost events of its kind in the world.

Every year, for three weeks in August, all eyes are on the dozens of performances in the many theatres of the city centre. Although the first festival was biased towards orchestral music, the modern programme is wide-ranging, with dance, music, opera and theatre. The city's ability to stage large-scale shows was considerably enhanced in 1994 with the development of the huge Edinburgh Festival Theatre, which has nearly two thousand seats and a stage larger than that of London's Royal Opera House. Details of the

The Fringe takes over the city every August

International Festival programme are available in March each year (www.eif.co.uk).

Edinburgh Festival Fringe

The Festival Fringe was born at the same time as the official festival and started as a sometimes irreverent, loose collection of additional performances held in the city. Initially, the Fringe consisted of several small theatre companies that were not included in the official programme but nevertheless decided to stage events on the same dates.

Free from the confines of the International Festival's rules and regulations, the Fringe has become synonymous with boundary-pushing art, specialising in experimental theatre and stand-up comedy. The event has grown to eclipse its sibling, selling about three million tickets a year. It comprises over 3800 different shows, with countless performances taking place at all times of the day and night in around 320 venues.

Every year the cream of young artistic and comic talent makes its way to Edinburgh, and the Fringe is arguably the largest showcase for performers in the world. A programme is produced in spring each year covering all the Fringe acts (www.edfringe.com).

Theatre and music

Of course you don't need to visit Edinburgh during the summer festivals in order to catch excellent performances of the arts in the city. World-class companies, including the National Theatre of Scotland, the Scottish Opera, Scottish Ballet, the Royal Scottish National Orchestra and the BBC Scottish Symphony Orchestra, all maintain busy programmes. There are also several major theatres with an ever-changing schedule of touring plays, ballets and musical performances, as well as popular shows featuring international singers and bands.

Although you will find venues scattered throughout the city, the main theatre district is found south of the west end of Princes Street. Off Lothian Road, the **Traverse Theatre** (10 Cambridge Street; www.traverse.co.uk) is Edinburgh's most exciting contemporary theatre, promoting new writing and emerging talent. Also in the vicinity, on Lothian Road, is the elegant concert venue **Usher Hall** (www.usherhall.co.uk). Nearby, on Grindlay Street, the **Royal Lyceum Theatre** (www.lyceum.org.uk) is a refurbished Victorian venue that stages high-quality classic and modern drama. The glass-fronted **Edinburgh Festival Theatre** on Nicolson Street (www.capitaltheatres.com/your-visit/festival-theatre)

NOTES

To find out what's on during your stay pop into a newsagent and buy a copy of *The List* magazine (www.list.co.uk).

plays an integral role in the International Festival, and is also the Edinburgh home to Scottish Opera and Scottish Ballet. West End musicals are put on in the East End-based **Playhouse Theatre** (18–22 Greenside Place; www.playhousetheatre.com).

Cinema

Filmgoers are well served in Edinburgh. The refurbished **Cameo** (38 Home Street; www.picturehouses.com) was first opened in 1914 and retains an original auditorium, screening art-house and commercial films. Another arty independent is the **Filmhouse** (88 Lothian Road; www.filmhousecinema.com), currently closed for renovation. For blockbusters and popcorn there's the twelve-screen **Vue** cinema at the Omni Centre (Greenside Place; www.myvue.com).

Ceilidhs

A number of companies offer an evening of Scottish dancing along with an 'addressing the haggis' ceremony – traditionally performed on Burns Night. You will find all the paraphernalia of kilts, bagpipes and ceremonial arms along with traditional Scottish food, whisky and dancing.

Regular *ceilidh* dances are held at the Assembly Roxy (2 Roxburgh Place; www.edinburghceilidhs.com), which are energetic and lots of fun. There is usually an experienced caller on hand to demonstrate the steps.

Nightlife

Edinburgh is a city with an energetic nightlife throughout the year, in part due to liberal licensing laws. Many bars close at midnight or later and clubs at about 3am. The best places to find late-night hangouts are Cowgate and Grassmarket in the Old Town, and Broughton Street and George Street in the New Town. Tucked away in the subterranean caverns beneath Cowgate is popular **Cabaret**

Voltaire (36–38 Blair Street; www.thecabaretvoltaire.com), while **Liquid Room** (9c Victoria Street; www.liquidroom.com) is one of the city's busiest.

Lulu (125b George Street; www.luluedinburgh.co.uk) is a club to remember, with crystals embedded in the walls. Descend the steps to **Bramble Bar** (16a Queen Street; www.bramblebar.co.uk), where cocktails are an art form, and rub elbows with the hippest of Edinburgh's drinking set.

For a classic city pub, try **The Guildford Arms** (www.guildford arms.com) on West Register Street, one block north of the east end of Princes Street. Grassmarket is a lively area for pubs, including the **The Last Drop**, another traditional drinking den, with low ceilings

Grassmarket at night

TRACING YOUR ANCESTORS

Edinburgh offers rich opportunities for the ancestor hunter. In New Register House, at the east end of Princes Street (just behind General Register House), there are records of every birth, marriage and death in Scotland since 1855; parish records date from even earlier. For a small charge, you can inspect the records and should be able to trace several generations (book in advance at www.scotlandspeople.gov.uk/visit-us).

Alternatively, you can try the Scottish Genealogy Society and Family History Centre, where non-members may take a research session (charge; 15 Victoria Terrace; www.scotsgenealogy.com).

If you don't want to attempt the task yourself, a private company that offers a free initial consultation is Scottish Roots Ancestral Research Service (16 Forth Street; www.scottishroots.com).

and low lighting. Its name is a reference to the gallows that used to stand in the square.

Shopping

Edinburgh draws the best of Scottish products to its shops and provides a ready marketplace for goods from the northern Highlands and islands. The major shopping street is Princes Street, where you'll find many major British names. Sadly, Edinburgh's traditional department store, Jenners, a local institution for generations, has now closed, though the ornate facade is a nod to its long-running legacy. The streets running parallel to Princes Street in the New Town, such as pedestrianised Rose Street and Thistle Street, are dotted with smaller shops and boutiques, while the upmarket George Street offers a range of designer fashion outlets, as does Multrees Walk (off St Andrew Square). Not to be overlooked, the knot of cobbled Georgian streets in Edinburgh's West End are lined by a delightful mix of designer boutiques, organic food stores and other independent shops.

At the top of the Royal Mile you'll find the typical tourist trappings, but duck down the narrow surrounding streets to discover one-off shops selling antiques, books and collectibles. For alternative fashion try Cockburn Street, which shoots off the High Street.

Covered Waverley Market is on Princes Street next to Waverley Railway Station, while the revamped St James Quarter is on Leith Street at the east end of Princes Street. Ocean Terminal at Leith waterfront also has excellent shopping.

What to buy

Tartan. This fabric is synonymous with Scotland – the major Scottish families had their own traditional tartan patterns that

Tartan products are ubiquitous

instantly identified their clan and kinship. If you have any Scottish ancestry, you will be able to find the tartan for you; otherwise, it is a matter of finding a design that you like. All new tartan patterns must be registered.

Traditionally tartans are worn in the form of a kilt or classic Highland dress. The Tartan Weaving Mill (see page 46) has about 170 tartans for sale but will also custom make a kilt for you to take home.

Woollens. The northern islands produce beautiful, heavy-knitted Fair Isle and Aran sweaters. After the Industrial Revolution cashmere was introduced to the weavers; the garments created from this wool make good gifts. Tweed is also produced from wool, and made into jackets, coats and suits.

Books. Edinburgh has long been at the forefront of publishing. It supported the work of the university, which was a major centre of learning from the sixteenth century, particularly in law, medicine and veterinary practice.

A legacy of the print industry is the number of bookshops selling second-hand, antiquarian and new books. Blackwell's (formerly James Thin) has the largest bookstore in Scotland (on South Bridge, opposite the university buildings of Chambers Street).

The city has a rich association with writers and authors, from Robert Louis Stevenson to Ian Rankin and JK Rowling, and in 2004 this literary legacy was honoured with UNESCO's first City of Literature designation.

Antiques. As a capital city, Edinburgh has its own office for the stamping of gold and silver, with the city's mark found on many antique pieces. If you find an old 'tappit hen' (a traditional drinking tankard), look for the silver assay mark of a castle, indicating an authentic Edinburgh design.

Jewellery, silver and other crafts. From the days of the Stuart kings, Scottish jewellery was known for the high quality of its workmanship. The use of traditional Scottish materials such as silver – and stones including carnelian or agate – makes for unique creations. Often, local Celtic patterns adorn bracelets, brooches and scarf rings. Classic craft skills also extend to the manufacture of high-quality pottery and glassware.

Outdoor activities

Golf. It is traditionally held that Scotland gave golf to the world, and the former Leith Links is considered the 'home of golf'. Around twenty courses participate in the Golf East Lothian scheme, which offers discount on 'stay and play' packages at some of the best golf courses in the area (www.scotlandsgolfcoast.com). It is advisable to book any course in advance.

Golf courses abound in East Lothian

NOTES

Football is a passion in Scotland. Edinburgh has two teams in the Premier League: Heart of Midlothian (Hearts), playing at Tynecastle Stadium, Gorgie Road (www.heartsfc.co.uk), and Hibernian (Hibs), who play at the Easter Road Stadium (www.hibernianfc.co.uk). Football season runs from August to mid-May.

Just 55 miles (88km) north of Edinburgh is St Andrews, a hallowed destination for golfers from around the world and one of the premier professional courses on the international tour. It is possible to play a round on a day excursion from Edinburgh, although it is difficult to book a starting time on the world-famous Old Course.

Rugby. Edinburgh is the home of Scottish Rugby Union. West of the city centre is Murrayfield Stadium, where Scottish and international games are held throughout the season, including the Calcutta Cup which pits the Scots against their 'auld' enemy the English. For tickets and information, visit www.scottishrugby.org.

Athletics. Meadowbank Stadium is the major venue for track and field athletics. It has a schedule of events in summer (www.edinburghleisure.co.uk/meadowbank2021).

Hillwalking. Holyrood Park, within the city's boundaries, provides an ideal area for walking, with fine views of Edinburgh from Arthur's Seat. The hike up this volcanic peak is steep but within the capability of an adequately fit person.

The Pentland Hills, which rise steeply on the southern tip of Edinburgh, provide some delightful hillwalking, the splendid views changing with the seasons.

Skiing. West of the city at Hillend is Midlothian Snow Sports Centre, the longest artificial ski slope in the UK (400 metres/1312ft). Open year round, the centre rents out equipment (www.midlothian.gov.uk). You will need to have some prior experience of skiing to use the slope; alternatively, lessons are offered.

Children's Edinburgh

Edinburgh has plenty of activities for children to enjoy. Take them to **Edinburgh Castle** (see page 39) for stories of heroism and marvellous city views. At Castlehill nearby, the **Camera Obscura** and **World of Illusions** (see page 46) are popular with children and offer a unique view of the city rooftops. Just be prepared for several flights of stairs to reach the top.

Explore the story of our planet at **Dynamic Earth** (see page 63). Here you can witness the Big Bang, experience an earth-quake and come face to face with a dinosaur all in one place.

Children will love seeing teddies, dolls, trains and pedal cars up-close at the **Museum of Childhood** (see page 53) and get hands-on with dressing-up costumes and games. Not for the very small or faint-hearted, **Edinburgh Dungeon** (www.thedungeons.com) offers an eye-opening journey through Scotland's murky past. **Edinburgh Zoo** (see page 85) in Corstorphine is a big draw for children. Over the Forth Road Bridge at North Queensferry, **Deep Sea World** (www.deepseaworld.com) is the site of Scotland's national aquarium. Its underwater tunnel offers a diver's-eye view of the deep.

Every May, the **Imaginate Children's Festival** (www.

Dynamic Earth

imaginate.org.uk) holds arts, theatre and dance activities and performances suitable for ages 8 to 15. The **Scottish Storytelling Centre** (see page 52) hosts weekly events throughout the year. During the festival, kids love the street theatre, clowns, face painting and temporary tattooing.

If your children are tired of trudging city streets, make sure to take a ride to **Portobello Beach** (on the Firth of Forth), where the long sprawling stretch of sand offers a perfect environment for walks, kite flying, or wading and swimming in the sea. It makes for a fun afternoon.

Festivals and events

It is no surprise that Edinburgh has an international reputation for being a festival city. Things reach fever pitch in August when there are no less than six major events, including the **International Festival** (see page 93) and the **Fringe** (see page 94). Other events worth coinciding a visit with include:

Burns Night: 25 January. Haggis, neeps and tatties and an 'address tae the haggis' is accompanied by the swirl of bagpipes as families and dedicated Burns societies settle down across the land to toast the birth of Rabbie Burns, the nation's most famous poet. www.rbwf.org.uk

International Children's Festival: Early May. A nine-day festival celebrates the best of children's theatre and dance from around the world. www.imaginate.org.uk/festival

Edinburgh International Book Festival: Last three weeks in August. Literary giants from around the world gather for readings, discussions, storytelling and book signings. Includes a much-praised children's programme. Held in Charlotte Square. www.edbookfest.co.uk

Edinburgh International Film Festival: Last two weeks in August. A prominent fixture in the film world featuring premieres, animations, documentaries, cult films and interviews. The main venue is the Filmhouse, with screenings around the city. www.edfilmfest.org.uk

Hogmanay fireworks

Edinburgh Jazz and Blues Festival: Mid-July. The best of national talent and visiting world-class jazz musicians. Various venues. www.edinburghjazzfestival.co.uk

Edinburgh International Science Festival: Two to three weeks in April. Catering for all levels of knowledge, there are plenty of hands-on experiments, exhibitions, events and lectures. www.sciencefestival.co.uk

Edinburgh Military Tattoo: Three weeks in August. Colourful displays of regimental marching, equestrianism and pipe-and-drum bands performed nightly on the Castle Esplanade. www.edintattoo.co.uk

Hogmanay: Three-day festival of torchlight parades, street theatre and food fairs to usher in the New Year. www.edinburghshogmanay.com

Food and drink

Edinburgh punches well above its weight in the gastronomy world. The dining scene is as diverse as the capital itself, thanks to exciting chefs, creative dining experiences and wide-ranging concepts, from fine dining to humble sandwich shops and much-loved neighbourhood restaurants. And people are catching on. The Scottish capital was named the Most Exciting Food Destination in 2025 by *The Good Food Guide* and, the same year, gained two more Michelin stars (*LYLA* and *Avery*; see pages 120 and 118), as well as two new Bib Gourmand winners (*Ardfern* and *Skua*; see page 121).

Culinary legacy

The Scots are proud of a cuisine distinct from that of the English, and they have contributed many fine ingredients to the British national palate of cooking styles. The clean air, pure water and acres of open lowlands and hills offer a bounty of fresh, local quality produce: from wild game and meats to fish, seafood, vegetables and fruit. Modern Scottish cooking uses the best of these ingredients, transforming them into inventive dishes bursting with flavour.

However, Edinburgh is not just a city of Scottish cuisine. A wide range of restaurants cater to different tastes, from Nepalese to Mexican and Middle Eastern. Varous districts are beginning to drum to their own culinary beat: Leith is famed for its creative, cool bars and award-winning restaurants, such as *Ardfern* and *Eleanore* (see page 119), while Stockbridge's fine-dining experiences – think

NOTES

The List's Eating and Drinking Guide provides listings for Edinburgh and Glasgow; www.list.co.uk. To find details of restaurants that serve traditional Scottish food, visit www.taste-of-scotland.com.

eòrna (see page 119) – cater to a well-heeled crowd. With seven establishments holding Michelin stars, Edinburgh can justifiably claim third place behind London and Birmingham in the UK's gourmand pecking order. A lively café culture has also taken the city centre by storm, including top-drawer coffee roasteries *Artisan Roast* and *Fortitude*.

Traditional Scottish fare

Top 10 things to eat

1. Soups and broths

Soups and thick broths have always been popular in Scotland, particularly in winter. Traditionally, cooks made a few ingredients go a long way, especially in poorer crofter families in the countryside. The internationally known Scotch broth comprises vegetable soup made with mutton stock and thickened with barley and lentils; cock-a-leekie is a soup of chicken and leeks (authentic only if it contains prunes). Popular seafood soups include cullen skink, a combination of smoked haddock, onions, potatoes and milk, and partan bree, cream of crab meat.

2. Haggis

The most famous Scottish dish, haggis was originally a dish for the poor, made from parts of the animal left after the major cuts had been taken. Haggis is traditionally made with the 'pluck' of a sheep: (the lungs, heart and liver); it's boiled for three hours, then the fat is skimmed off and the rest minced. Oatmeal, onion, seasoning, spices and gravy add flavour, and the entire mixture is stuffed into a sheep's 'paunch' or stomach (modern haggis may be encased in an artificial skin to avoid bursting). The filled skin is then simmered in water for up to two hours. Served piping hot, the haggis is cut lengthwise and the meat mixture scooped out (the casing is discarded). It is typically eaten with neeps and tatties (mashed turnip and mashed potatoes).

NOTES

If you fancy a light bite or a restorative round of tea and cake, Edinburgh has an abundant supply of cafés. The Elephant House (21 George IV Bridge; closed for restoration until at least 2023 following a fire) was where JK Rowling drank coffee and dreamt up Harry Potter. Union of Genius (8 Forrest Road) serves six different soups a day, and Clarinda's (69 Canongate) also serves tasty home-made food. For great Italian coffee, try Valvona and Crolla (19 Elm Row).

3. Fish and seafood

Scottish fish and shellfish is the envy of Europe, with everything from prawns, lobsters and mussels to oysters, crab and scallops found around the extensive coastline. However, catches from the nearby seas and rivers have been diminishing. Salmon was, until recently, a fish available only to rich landowners, caught in private rivers. Smoked sea fish such as haddock or herring were traditionally on a working-class menu, produced in smoking sheds along the coast of the Firth of Forth before being transported to the residential areas of the city. Today, class lines have been blurred and the most modest of fish dishes have become fashionable. River salmon and trout remain expensive, but the supply has been supplemented in recent years by farmed fish (though aficionados will argue that the taste is not the same as wild fish).

Smoked salmon can be enjoyed as an appetiser with bread and butter, or the whole fish might be poached as a starter. You will also find finan haddie or Arbroath smokies (line-caught haddock smoke-cured over smouldering oak chips).

4. Sweet treats

The Scots are known for their sweet tooth. Wild fruits from the land – raspberries, blackberries, rhubarb and gooseberries, among others – form the basis of many pies and puddings, often with a crisp coating of oatmeal. Cranachan is a dish of raspberries and cream topped with toasted oatmeal. Atholl Brose is a delicious blend of whisky, honey, cream and oatmeal – a rather adult version of

Alfresco eating and drinking in summer – weather permitting

Delicacies at the National Galleries of Scotland: Modern café

porridge. Auld Alliance, creamed cheese laced with whisky, is traditionally eaten as a spread on toasted bread.

5. Cheese

Cheese can also be found in great variety, served with oatcakes. Try Dunlop, not unlike cheddar; Lanark Blue, a Roquefort-style blue cheese; or Bonchester, a Camembert-style offering.

6. Shortbread

Shortbread was originally an oatmeal bread served at Christmas, though it was a food carried over from pagan times. Made in a circle and pinched around the edge with the finger, it was meant to symbolise the rays of the sun that would bring rebirth to the land in spring. The oatmeal was subsequently replaced by finer milled flour to create today's shortbread biscuit, which is rich in sugar and butter.

7. Meat and game

Scottish-reared beef is considered world-class, especially the Aberdeen Angus breed, though Highland cattle are also rated for their depth of flavour. The local lamb is also excellent. Venison, the meat of the red deer, is also popular with Scots – low in cholesterol and very tasty, it's served roasted or in casseroles, and is often cooked with juniper and red wine. Other forms of game include grouse, which when cooked properly is strong, dark and succulent; pheasant, a lighter meat; and the less commonly served, but still tasty, pigeon and rabbit.

8. Full Scottish breakfast

A full Scottish breakfast will always include bacon, sausage, black pudding (blood sausage), eggs, tomatoes, mushrooms and toast. Juice and cereal will also be a part of the full shebang. If this is a little too much to eat first thing in the morning, lighter traditional dishes include smoked kippers from Loch Fyne or finan haddie (fillet of haddock smoked with peat) poached in milk. Kedgeree is another nutritious option, consisting of a delicious mixture of flaked fish, rice and hard-boiled eggs.

9. Clootie dumpling

A traditional dessert in Scotland, the humble clootie dumpling is a sweet, stodgy fruit pudding bound in a cloth and cooked for hours.

NOTES

Fair fa' your honest,
sonsie face,
Great chieftain o' the
puddin'-race!
Aboon them a' ye tak
your place,
Painch, tripe, or thairm:
Weel are ye wordy of a grace
As lang's my arm.
– Robert Burns (1786)

A classic Scottish dish: haggis, neeps and tatties

10. Porridge

The classic, unassuming breakfast staple – and a soul-nourishing one at that. Porridge is properly made with oatmeal and water, and cooked with a pinch of salt. Some prefer to add milk and honey, fruit or sugar to sweeten.

When to eat

In restaurants lunch is typically eaten from noon to 2.30pm, though many pubs serve food all day. Set lunches are a good deal, and many places offer them Monday to Friday. You will also find numerous sandwich bars and cafés. There are good cafés in Edinburgh Castle, the National Museum of Scotland and the National Galleries of Scotland: Portrait. High tea, generally served between 3pm and 5pm, is often a lavish affair.

Dinner is normally taken from 6.30pm to 10.30pm, but most restaurants serve later on weekends and during the summer season. Many, including some of the more renowned, will offer pre- or post-theatre special menus, serving early or late depending on your needs. These are very popular – especially during the festival season – so you should book tables in advance.

The whisky scene

Without doubt, the king of Scottish drinks is whisky, a concoction that the Scots are said to have invented, though the Irish might dispute that. Whisky – *uisge beatha*, the 'water of life' in Gaelic – has been produced in Scotland since the fifteenth century, but only really took off after the 1780 tax on claret made wine too expensive for most people. The taxman soon caught up with whisky, however, and drove the stills underground. Today, many distilleries operate on the site of simple cottages that once distilled the stuff illegally.

Single malts

Despite the dominance of blended whiskies such as Johnnie Walker, Bell's, Teacher's and The Famous Grouse, single malt whisky is infinitely superior and, as a result, a great deal more expensive. Single malts are produced from malted barley and bottled direct from the barrel, and each of the several hundred produced by different distilleries in Scotland has a distinctive taste. They vary in character enormously depending on the amount of peat used for drying the barley, the water used for mashing and the type of oak cask used in the maturing process. Lowland malts (from the area in the south of Scotland) are softer in style and flavour; Speyside malts (from farther north, east of Inverness) are considered the 'cream' of single malt; Highland and island malts (Islay, Arran, Jura, Skye, Mull) are

HIGH TEA

The prim ladies for whom Edinburgh is famed – in the style of Miss Jean Brodie – would shop in town and take tea at one of the fine hotels or cafés as a finale to their afternoon. This tradition continues, a perfect activity for visitors to sit and relax in a genteel environment after a day of sightseeing (between 3pm and 5pm). In addition to the sandwiches and cream cakes, you may be tempted by a potato scone, or a slice of Dundee cake (a rich fruitcake decorated with almonds), or a black bun (a cake flavoured with dried fruit ginger mixed with cinnamon and brandy). Jams and honey made with produce from the countryside are a delicious accompaniment.

unique in their flavour, sometimes heavy with heather peat, producing a 'medicinal' taste.

Malt whisky is aged for a number of years in oak barrels before being bottled; the minimum time is three years, but some are aged for fifteen or twenty. Ageing refines the taste and imparts the distinctive colour to the whisky. Malt whisky is best drunk with a splash of water to release its distinctive flavours.

The nearest working distillery to the city, Glenkinchie, produces a very soft lowland malt, a perfect introduction to single malts. Distillery tours are available (www.malts.com/en-row/distilleries/glenkinchie). Most bars stock a range of malts and blended whiskies to try, and the shops in the Scotch Whisky Experience and Johnnie Walker Princes Street have an extensive range – including many rare and unusual examples – from all parts of Scotland.

Blended whisky

In the past both the quality and quantity of whisky production would vary, and the flavour of many single malts was not suited to the taste of the mass population. In the eighteenth century, a group of distillers decided to create a standard product that could be produced in batches for consistency and palatability. They began to produce whisky from grains other than malted barley and to mix different whiskies (malts and non-malts) together, producing the blended whiskies of today.

Blends contain whiskies of different ages – up to forty different whiskies in one blend. When a blend has an age on the label, it is the age of the youngest whisky in the blend.

The art of whisky blenders is a fine one. They smell different aged whiskies to

NOTES

Whisky is generally served neat, with ice or with a little water. If you drink it with soda water, you might get a friendly lecture from a Scot.

create a blend, very much as a perfumer creates a fragrance. Only a few individuals have the 'nose' for the job, and this has often been a hereditary occupation, passed down from father to son or daughter.

There are over seven hundred pubs in Edinburgh

Drambuie

Drambuie was said to be Bonnie Prince Charlie's favourite drink. He bequeathed its secret recipe to his friend MacKinnon of Straithard in gratitude for organising the prince's escape from the English army in 1746. The drink was made in small quantities for family consumption until 1909, when it went on general sale. The MacKinnon family continued to keep the recipe a secret while making a success of the commercial production. Interestingly, the recipe was passed down through the female line of the family.

After a hundred years of ownership, in September 2014 Drambuie was sold to William Grant & Sons.

Glayva

First produced in 1940, *glayva* (meaning 'very good') blends whisky, herbal oils, honey and sugar. Ronald Morrison and George Petrie, a chemist, worked together at their Leith blending works to perfect the taste and flavour. To preserve the secrecy of the drink, the recipe is known by only three people at any one time.

Places to eat

Each restaurant and café reviewed in this Guide is accompanied by a price category, based on the cost of a three-course meal (or similar) for one, excluding drinks:

££££ = over £45

£££ = £35–45

££ = £25–35

£ = below £25

Old town

Amber Restaurant The Scotch Whisky Experience, 354 Castlehill, Royal Mile, www.scotchwhiskyexperience.co.uk/restaurant. Lunch here is informal and good value, with delicious tapas and sandwiches alongside heartier mains. For dinner, first-rate service is accompanied by an innovative menu including Scottish estate-bred beef and prime lamb, as well as the freshest loch and North Sea fish. **££**

Angels with Bagpipes 343 High Street, www.angelswithbagpipes.co.uk. Contemporary style meets Old Town at this delightful restaurant close to St Giles Cathedral. Top-class chefs create original menus based on Scotland's finest food larder. **£££**

Daika Kurdish Grill 3 Johnston Terrace, www.daika.co.uk. Middle-Eastern and Kurdish cooking, such as shish kebabs – Iranian or Kurdish style – chargrills and vegetarian options. No alcohol but there is a good range of non-alcoholic wines, beers and ciders. **££**

David Bann's Vegetarian Restaurant 56–58 St Mary's Street, www.davidbann.co.uk. A popular restaurant serving an excellent range of vegetarian dishes from around the globe to a mixed clientele, from Edinburgh students and locals to visitors. **££**

Luckenbooths 329 High Street, https://luckenboothsedinburgh.co.uk. Named after the locked booths inside the tenement buildings that once stood here on the Royal Mile, *Luckenbooths* is a family-friendly restaurant celebrating Scotland's local larder. The all-day menu includes beetroot-glazed Scottish smoked salmon with dill crème fraîche and rye toast, and haggis and beef-shin bonbons. Soak up the historic surroundings from the outside terrace. **££**

Museum Brasserie At the Museum of Scotland, 18–27 Chambers Street. With exposed brick and stone arches, the cellar-like *Museum Brasserie* has an extensive menu offering hot and cold lunches, freshly prepared sandwiches, home baking and children's boxes. **£**

Namaste Kathmandu 17/19 Forrest Road, www.namastektm.co.uk. Authentic, delicious Indian and Nepalese cuisine can be found a few yards away from the National Museum. Many tasty dishes served in a moodily lit atmosphere. **££**

Timberyard 10 Lady Lawson Street, www.timberyard.co. Located in a former warehouse, this family business is about respecting the environment. Only ingredients made by local artisanal growers and makers go into imaginative dishes, and some produce comes from the on-site kitchen-garden. Dishes include the likes of sea bass served with mussels, sea beet and vermouth, or caramelised pork belly nestled among buttery cabbage, kimchi and salted apple. The team are a dab hand in pickling, curing and foraging, so expect plent of home-made delights. **£££**

Wedgewood the Restaurant 267 Canongate, www.wedgwoodtherestaurant.co.uk. Using the best home-grown ingredients, many foraged or grown locally, this Royal Mile establishment creates fabulous Scottish dishes bursting with flavour, such as spiced monkfish served with crab bhaji, and loin of venison. Plenty of vegan and vegetarian dishes available. **£££**

The Witchery by the Castle 352 Castlehill, Royal Mile, www.thewitchery.com. Set just below the castle esplanade, this pair of two historic dining rooms are striking in their splendour and illuminated only by candlelight at night. Surrounded by fluted columns, tasselled curtains and marble busts, diners feast on the likes of oysters followed by roast guinea fowl, lemon sole or Scotch beef fillet. Not a cheap affair, but worth it for a special occasion. Good-value pre- and post-theatre suppers are available. **£££**

New Town

Avery 54 St Stephen Street, www.averyedi.co.uk. American chef Rodney Wages has brought a slice of Californian cool to Edinburgh, moving his boundary-pushing restaurant *Avery* from the streets of San Francisco via shipping container to a Georgian townhouse in Stockbridge. And it paid off: this British reincarnation garnered a Michelin star in 2025. Drawing on the natural larder of Scotland, the menu gives bold flavours a playful touch in dishes like Orkney scallop in a pineapple jus or oyster cream served with a dumpling, caviar lava and anchovy jelly. **££££**

The Bon Vivant 55–57 Thistle Street, www.bonvivantedinburgh.co.uk. This low-lit restaurant is a popular evening hangout for Scottish cuisine with a modern spin. Enjoy small plates of haggis bon bons and venison pasties, followed by slow-roasted pork belly or rump steak with red-wine truffle sauce. **££**

Browns 131–133 George Street, www.browns-restaurants.co.uk. Art Deco-styled gem with high ceilings, black-and-white tiled floors and opulent gold finishes. The menu features classic British dishes and fresh seasonal creations, as well as afternoon tea. **£££**

Contini Ristorante 103 George Street, www.contini.com. Northern Italian flavours abound in this classy, tiled former bank turned bistro, slap bang in the city centre. Formerly known as the *Centotre*, it is still run by the same family and continues to serve delicious food, as well as coffees and cocktails. **££**

Dean Banks at the Pompadour *Waldorf Astoria – The Caledonian*, Princes Street, www.deanbanks.co.uk. Dean Banks has brought his culinary genius to Edinburgh's most elegant and formal dining room. The evolving menu reflects the seasons and Scotland's natural resources. Guests enjoy a sensory experience that will leave a lasting memory. **££££**

Dusit 49a Thistle Street, www.dusit.co.uk. Delivering some of the most consistently good food and service in Edinburgh, *Dusit* sets the bar high for Thai cuisine with its contemporary, perfectly executed dishes. **££**

Eleanore 30–31 Albert Place, www.eleanore.uk. Season-led cuisine is in the spotlight at *Eleanore*, a brilliant white space broken up with the odd pickle-laden shelf. Chef Roberta Hall masterminded the menu, conjuring up creations like asparagus and wild garlic hash browns or crab croustade with cucumber and bearnaise. Come for the set lunch to score a £40 bargain or arrive later in the evening for £70 tasting menus – a steal, mind you, considering the quality. **£££**

eòrna 68 Hamilton Place, https://eornarestaurant.com. This small, twelve-seat haunt features just counter seating at a curved marble bar, where chef Brian Grigor plonks plates of Orkney beef or North Sea cod loin in front of loyal patrons, paired with excellent wines recommended by in-the-know sommelier Glen Montgomery. A fun and intimate dining experience. **£££**

L'Escargot Bleu 56 Broughton Street, www.lescargotbleu.co.uk. Behind its attractive blue facade, this engaging brasserie is plastered with French posters and helmed by friendly staff. The food is classic French with one exception: it's made using the very best Scottish produce. **££**

Gusto 135 George Street, www.gustorestaurants.uk.com. A modern, open-kitchen Italian restaurant with industrial-style decor and a bustling atmosphere: a typical *trattoria* with a modern twist. Expect all the usual classics, from bruschetta, thin-crust pizza and pasta dishes to risotto, grilled meats and tiramisu. **££**

LYLA 3 Royal Terrace, https://lylaedinburgh.co.uk. For a blowout meal, you won't find anything quite as exacting as *LYLA* anywhere else in Edinburgh. And it has a Michelin star to prove it. Helmed by restaurant titan Stuart Ralston, of *Aizle* fame, the menu focuses on sustainably sourced and foraged ingredients. The results: a sublime tasting menu (£165) spanning ten courses of culinary delights, such as Scottish langoustine with burnt apple and sorrel, or wagyu with marrow, crispy onions and pickled walnut. Expensive yes, but worth the splurge. **££££**

The Magnum 1 Albany Street, https://themagnumrestaurant.co.uk. The chefs here use fresh, local ingredients to create Scottish dishes such as cullen skink and haggis, alongside game, beef and seafood plates. **££**

Number One 1 Princes Street (at *The Balmoral* hotel), www.roccofortehotels.com/hotels-and-resorts/the-balmoral-hotel. The restaurant oozes panache without being pompous. Culinary treats could include Balmoral smoked salmon with quails' egg and caviar or Borders' roe deer, rainbow chard, sausage, hazelnuts and pistachio. They are all complemented by a fine wine list. Open Thursday–Monday for dinner only. **££££**

The Palmerston 1 Palmerston Place, www.thepalmerstonedinburgh.co.uk. Housed in a former bank, *The Palmerston* has a relaxed vibe and minimalist decor. Seasonal menus showcase produce from the best suppliers across Scotland, and there is an in-house bakery and coffee shop. **££**

Pickles 56a Broughton Street, www.getpickled.co.uk. Located beneath *L'Escargot Bleu* (see page 119), this quirky little place is ideal for a light bite and a drink. Delicious platters piled high with Scottish cheeses or meat come with, naturally, a huge range of pickles and sides. £

Skua 49 St Stephen Street, www.skua.scot. Fine dining and fried chicken aren't usually muttered in the same breath, but *Skua* isn't your usual haunt. With moody walls and flickering candlelight, this atmospheric setting is the place to go for rustic sharing plates. Of course, don't miss the signature fried chicken drizzled with peach hot sauce but save room for the doughnuts with smoked cheese and guanciale or the hispi cabbage and kombu. **£££**

Stac Polly 29–33 Dublin Street, www.stacpolly.com. The award-winning *Stac Polly* has garnered a reputation throughout the city for exciting Scottish dishes made with local ingredients. The traditional setting in a labyrinth of cellars adds to a real Scottish evening. There is also a brasserie and gin and wine bar upstairs for more relaxed dining. **£££**

Valvona and Crolla 19 Elm Row, www.valvonacrolla.co.uk. A charming Italian restaurant tucked away to the back of a fabled deli. Prepared fresh to order, using traditional methods and the finest Scottish and Italian ingredients. Pick from light bites or more substantial fresh fish and meat dishes. **££**

Wildfire 192 Rose Street, www.wildfirerestaurant.co.uk. Chargrilled Aberdeen Angus steaks are a highlight here, along with the changing seafood menu featuring dishes such as dressed white crab with lime crème fraîche and fisherman's pie. **££**

Leith

Ardfern 10–12 Bonnington Road, www.ardfern.uk. Named after a village in Argyll and Bute that recalls fond memories for owner Roberta Hall-McCarron, *Ardfern* is an inviting café, bar and bottle shop that's garnered a Bib Gourmand for its efforts. Arrive early for brunch, stay late for small plates and exciting wine choices; don't miss the hash browns with whipped feta and jalapeño ketchup. **£££**

Fishers Leith 1 The Shore, www.fishersrestaurants.co.uk. A compact, homely seafood restaurant looking out over the Water of Leith. Try the Anstruther langoustine tails or Shetland hake fillet. **££**

Heron 91A Henderson Street, www.heron.scot. Modern Scottish restaurant masterminded by Sam Yorke, with a Michelin star under its belt. Playful dishes on the seasonal menu might include the likes of Orkney scallops with ponzu or catch of the day. You'll have to dig deep for this dining experience, but it's worth it. **££££**

The Kitchin 78 Commercial Quay, www.thekitchin.com. This top-end Michelin-starred restaurant, headed up by Tom Kitchin, operates the philosophy 'nature to plate'. Maybe start with hand-dived Orkney scallops, follow with roasted loin of roe deer and finish with a delectable rum baba. **££££**

The Little Chartroom 14 Bonnington Road, www.thelittlechartroom.com. A much-loved neighbourhood bistro with unpretentious surroundings and an unassuming but delicious menu. Order crab anolini in a pool of tomato broth followed by stuffed hake or barbecue hispi. Save room for the plum bakewell tart accompanied by a dollop of treacle ice cream. **£££**

Roseleaf 23/24 Sandport Place, www.roseleaf.co.uk. Quirky family-run bar-café with a lively atmosphere and great home-cooked food, from spiced lamb kofta to beetroot burger. Wide range of drinks and cocktails served in teapots. **£**

Shore Bar and Restaurant 3 Shore, www.fishersrestaurants.co.uk. This historic hostelry prides itself on its seafood. For a cheaper, more casual option try the *Shore Bar*. Live jazz music several times each week. **££**

Travel essentials

Practical information

Accessible travel

Edinburgh is an old city; installing ramps, lifts, wide doorways and accessible toilets is, unfortunately, impossible in many of the city's older and historic buildings. Access has improved, however, with some of the city's most iconic attractions – including Edinburgh Castle, the Palace of Holyrood House and the Scottish Parliament – relatively accessible. Some hotels and a handful of B&Bs have one or two adapted rooms, usually on the ground floor and with step-free showers, grab rails and wider doorways. Most trains in Scotland have wheelchair lifts, and assistance is, in theory, available at all manned stations – see www.scotrail.co.uk/plan-yourjourney/accessible-travel. Wheelchair-users (alone or with a companion) and blind or partially sighted people (with a companion only) are automatically given thirty to fifty percent reductions on train fares. For more information and advice, contact the disability charity Capability Scotland (https://www.capability.scot).

Accommodation (see also Camping and Youth hostels)

Edinburgh offers an extensive range of accommodation: luxury and boutique hotels, historic houses, more modest hotels, boarding houses, simple bed-and-breakfast establishments, backpackers' hostels and campus accommodation. Should you wish to stay for a substantial period of time, there are also self-catering options usually available on a weekly basis, as well as more expensive serviced apartments. VisitScotland (the Scottish Tourist Board; www.visitscotland.com) produces an e-brochure listing an extensive range of accommodation in Edinburgh and the Lothians, with everything from hotels and self-catering to more unusual accommodation such as glamping or aboard a boat.

Hotels and guesthouses that have been independently inspected and approved by VisitScotland are given ratings according to the quality of the accommodation. Star gradings range from one star (fair and acceptable) to five stars (exceptional/world class).

In the high season (July–September), and especially in August during the month of the Edinburgh Festivals, the city becomes particularly crowded, and rooms are at a premium. Hogmanay (December and early January) is another busy time. Should you intend to visit during these periods, you are strongly advised to book accommodation as far in advance as possible.

In publicity materials, prices for rooms are usually quoted for a double room per night. Breakfast is usually included, but do check before making a reservation. Rooms in most hotels have en suite bathrooms, but some B&Bs (particularly at the budget end of the market) may have shared facilities. Always make sure you know what is included in the price of the room. VAT is always included in the price, but service charges (between ten and fifteen percent) might not be. Many hotels, however, do not add this charge.

For those on a budget who do not want to stay in a backpackers' hostel, all three Edinburgh universities offer accommodation in their halls of residence over holiday times. This is cheaper than most hotels but not always cheaper than a B&B in a private house. The University of Edinburgh is the most central (https://www.uoecollection.com), offering en-suite double rooms from around £55–60, some with views of Arthur's Seat. There's also Napier University (www.napier.ac.uk) and Heriot Watt University (www.hw.ac.uk).

Airports (see also Getting there)

Edinburgh International Airport (www.edinburghairport.com) lies seven miles (11km) west of the city. In addition to receiving flights from airports throughout Britain and other European destinations, a few non-stop flights land here from the US. British Airways runs comprehensive services to Edinburgh from London Heathrow and City airports. EasyJet operates low-cost flights from London Gatwick, Luton and Stansted, while Ryanair flies from Dublin. Airlink #100 shuttle bus connects the airport with the city (Waverley Bridge) around every ten minutes (every twenty minutes during the night) at a cost of £4.50 one way, £7.50 return, and takes between thirty and forty minutes depending on traffic. A night bus (#22) also runs. A tram also runs every seven minutes between 7am and 7pm (every fifteen minutes outside these hours) from the airport to the city (Picardy Place), at a cost of £6.50 one way, £9 return. Metred taxis cost £25–30. Airport Transfers

Direct (http://airport-transfers-direct.com) offers fixed-price taxis at a flat rate of £44 to the city centre, with travel time around 35 minutes, and they are available from just outside the East Terminus.

Glasgow International Airport (www.glasgowairport.com) is just over an hour's drive from Edinburgh. Frequent buses link the airport to the city centre (£8.50 one way, £14 return). Trains to Edinburgh from Queen Street Station run every five to ten minutes during the day, taking 55 minutes (approx £14 one way off peak). Frequent buses run to Edinburgh from Buchanan Street bus station taking about 1hr 20min (approximately £3.60 one-way).

For bus and rail travel information in Scotland contact Traveline (www.travelinescotland.com).

Apps

An essential app to make travelling around the Scottish capital a breeze is the **Transport for Edinburgh** app; download your bus or tram tickets straight to your mobile. History buffs should look into the **Edinburgh World Heritage City** app, which is an essential guide to the UNESCO and historic gems of the city. Active types might be interested in **Edinburgh Outdoors** for its information on the green spaces and urban parks in the area.

Bicycle hire

Despite being a hilly city, Edinburgh takes care of its cyclists, offering cycle paths and allowing cyclists to use separate bus lanes in the city centre. For rental, try Cycle Scotland, 29 Blackfriars Street (http://cyclescotland.co.uk). Local cycling action group Spokes (http://spokes.org.uk) publishes an excellent map of the city with recommended cycle routes. Cyclists can also take advantage of the Old Town's narrow alleyways, where cars are not allowed to travel.

Budgeting for your trip

Britain is a relatively expensive place to visit. Here are a few guidelines to help with budget-planning:

Accommodation: £150–180 for a double room, including breakfast, per night in a medium hotel.
Meals: Three-course dinner £50–60 per person in a moderate restaurant with wine.
Domestic airfare: From £140 (roundtrip/return) from London Heathrow to Edinburgh.
Car hire: £280 per week (£70 per day) for a medium-sized vehicle, including VAT and unlimited mileage, but not insurance.
Attractions, museums and galleries: From £10 to £20 for an adult; many city museums and galleries are free.
Theatre tickets: £30–40 for a mid-price ticket.
Bus tour of the city: £18.

Car hire

If you plan to spend most of your time in Edinburgh's compact city centre a vehicle will probably be more of a hindrance than a help, as parking is difficult. However, if you plan to take trips into the surrounding countryside, you will want to hire a car.

All major car-hire companies have desks at Edinburgh's airport (**Arnold Clark**, tel: 0131 357 2180, www.arnoldclarkrental.com; **Avis**, tel: 0344 544 6004, www.avis.co.uk; **Europcar**, tel: 0371 384 3406, www.europcar.co.uk; **Hertz**, tel: 0843 309 3025, www.hertz.co.uk; **Enterprise**, tel: 0131 333 0400, www.nationalcar.co.uk), and it is possible to pick up a car immediately upon your arrival in the city. If you are visiting from outside the UK, it can be cheaper to reserve your car from home rather than when you arrive.

Many companies have a minimum age (usually 21) for drivers, and you will need to have your full licence (with at least a year's driving experience) when you pick up the car. Credit cards are the preferred method of payment. Insurance covers collision damage and theft, but you may have to pay an excess.

Climate

Southern Scotland has a temperate climate influenced by its proximity to the Atlantic Ocean, though Edinburgh in particular is affected by the North

Sea. The summers are warm and wet; the winters are cold and wet. Even in summer, cold spells can occur and the weather can change quickly.

Average monthly temperatures are as follows:

	J	F	M	A	M	J	J	A	S	O	N	D
°C	4	5	7	10	14	17	19	18	15	11	7	6
°F	39	41	44	50	58	62	66	64	59	52	44	43

Crime and safety (see also Emergencies)

The centre of Edinburgh is fairly safe compared to other large European cities. All the same, you should take the usual precautions against theft. Any theft or loss must be reported immediately to the police in order to comply with your travel insurance. If your passport is lost or stolen, you should also inform your consulate.

City streets are relatively busy. This makes walking safe, but always make sure that you walk in well-lit streets late at night.

Customs and entry requirements

Entry requirements. From April 2025, European visitors to the UK require an Electronic Travel Authorisation (ETA), including those previously eligible for visa-free travel. This includes EU and EEA nationals. The ETA is required for short stays of up to six months.

Citizens of Australia, Canada, New Zealand, South Africa and the US need only a valid passport to enter the UK for tourist visits of up to six months. All passports must be valid for six months beyond the intended length of stay in the UK.

Upon arrival you will have to complete an entry card stating the address where you will be staying. The immigration officer will stamp your passport, allowing you to stay in Britain for a specific length of time. If your plans are uncertain, ask for several months so you don't have to apply for an extension later. Provided you have sufficient funds to cover your stay, there should not be a problem.

Your best starting point for a visa-related enquiry concerning entry to the UK is to contact the UK Foreign and Commonwealth Offices visa website (www.gov.uk/visas-immigration).

Currency. There are no currency restrictions when entering or leaving the UK, for either British or foreign currencies.

Driving (see also Car hire)

If you are bringing your own car or one from Europe, you will need the registration papers and insurance coverage. The usual formula is the Green Card, an extension to existing insurance that validates it for other countries. Don't forget your driver's licence.

Rules and regulations. Remember to drive on the left. Pay special attention at crossings and roundabouts. Traffic that is already in the roundabout has the right of way over cars waiting to enter the roundabout, and the rule is to give way to the right.

Drivers and passengers must use seat belts. Motorcycle riders must wear a crash helmet, and a driver's licence is required for all types of motorcycle. The minimum age for mopeds is 16 years, and 17 for motorcycles and scooters.

In built-up areas the speed limit, unless indicated to the contrary, is 30mph (48kmh); on motorways 70mph (112kmh); and on other inter-city roads 60mph (96kmh), except when these are dual carriageways when it is 70mph (112kmh). The prevailing speed limit is posted on road signs at the side of the road.

Edinburgh has a number of special lanes for buses and taxis only. These usually operate 7.30–9.30am and 4–6.30pm, easing the traffic flow at peak times. One-way streets also help to prevent bottlenecks. If you plan to drive around the city, invest in a good map.

Road conditions. There are three main types of roads: motorways (expressways), A roads (trunk roads that link all the major towns) and B roads (rural roads). Driving conditions in the UK are generally very good, and all A roads are of good quality.

Fuel costs. Petrol is expensive in the UK: approximately £1.45–£1.50 per litre. Most garages have self-service pumps, all of which give measurements in litres. You will find stations in all major towns. The normal hours of operation are 7am–10pm, but this can vary enormously. Some petrol stations are open 24 hours a day.

Parking. You can park at the side of the street provided there are no restrictions. Many streets will have areas for resident parking with fines for those who break the rules. Street parking is expensive, with costs of £4–6 per hour. Both street parking and car parks throughout the city operate a 'Pay and Display' system – you purchase a ticket from a machine and display the ticket on your dashboard.

Assistance. Most hire cars come with coverage from a reputable recovery or breakdown service. The Automobile Association (AA), the Royal Automobile Club (RAC) and Green Flag are well known.

Road signs. Britain has the same basic system of pictographs in use throughout Europe. The *Highway Code* is the official booklet of road usage and signs, available at most bookshops.

Electricity

The standard electrical supply in the UK is 240 volts AC, 50 Hz. All visitors (except South Africans) will need an adapter (with square 3-pin plugs) for any appliance brought from home, as well as a converter unless the appliance is equipped with one. Adapters are available at airport shops. Most hotels have special sockets for shavers and hairdryers that operate on 240 or 110 volts.

Embassies, consulates and high commissions

Many countries have consuls or other representatives in Edinburgh, but others have representation only in London.

Australia: Australian High Commission, Australia House, Strand, London WC2B 4LA, tel: 020 7379 4334.

Canada: Canadian High Commission, Canada House, Trafalgar Square, London SW1Y 5BJ, tel: 020 7004 6000.

Ireland: Consulate General of Ireland, 16 Randolph Crescent, Edinburgh EH3 7TT, tel: 226 7711.

New Zealand: New Zealand Consulate, 5 Rutland Square, Edinburgh EH1 2AS, tel: 222 8109.
South Africa: South African High Commission, South Africa House, Trafalgar Square, London WC2N 5DP, tel: 020 7451 7299.
US: American Consulate General, 3 Regent Terrace, Edinburgh EH7 5BW, tel: 556 8315.

Emergencies (see also Health and medical care and Police)

The emergency telephone number throughout the UK is **999**.

Getting there (see also Airports)

By rail. Conveniently situated at the eastern end of Princes St, right in the heart of the city, Waverley Station (http://nationalrail.co.uk) is the arrival point for all mainline trains. From central London and the London airports there are rail links (through King's Cross Station) to Waverley Station run by London North Eastern Railway (www.lner.co.uk). The journey takes about 4hr 30min–5hr. Contact National Rail Enquiries (www.nationalrail.co.uk), www.scotrail.co.uk or www.raileurope.com for details of this and other British and European train travel. There's a second mainline train stop, Haymarket Station, just under two miles west on the lines from Waverley to Glasgow, Fife and the Highlands, although this is only really of use if you're staying nearby.
By bus. National Express offers a comprehensive network of coach/bus services throughout the UK, with regular service from London's Victoria Station to Edinburgh. You can connect as well via other cities and towns as part of an itinerary. Further details and timetables are available by phone in the UK only (www.nationalexpress.com). For local bus (and rail) travel information in Scotland contact Traveline (www.travelinescotland.com). The bus and coach terminal for intercity services is located on the east side of St Andrew Square, a 2min walk from Waverley Station.
By car. Edinburgh is in the north of the UK, reached from England either directly via the A1 (in the east) or via the M6 (in the west); the M6 connects with the M74 and then the A702 to reach Edinburgh. The driving time is approximately seven hours on either route, depending on traffic and weather.

From Ireland, Irish Ferries (www.irishferries.com) offers ferry crossings from Dublin to Holyhead, Wales; from there, take the M6 for the onward drive to Edinburgh. Ferry services from Northern Ireland operate from Larne and Belfast to Cairnyan.

Guides and tours

There are several types of tours in the Edinburgh region. Themed walking tours are a great favourite. Options include:

Auld Reekie Tours (www.auldreekietours.com). Four macabre tours, with a focus on ghost stories, town history and jovial banter, delving into Edinburgh's narrow closes and vaults, one of which contains a torture exhibition.

The Real Mary King's Close see page 52.

The Edinburgh Literary Pub Tour (www.edinburghliterarypubtour.co.uk). Tours through the Old Town mixing a pub crawl with commentary by local costumed actors depicting literary characters. It's a fun way to explore Edinburgh's finest drinking dens while being introduced to the scenes, characters and words of the major figures of Scottish literature, including Burns, Scott, and MacDiarmid. Begins at 7.30pm at the *Beehive Inn* in the Grassmarket. Runs May–Sept daily; Jan–March Fri and Sun; April and Oct Thurs–Sun; Nov–Dec Fri only.

Invisible Edinburgh (www.invisible-cities.org). Walking tours showcasing an idiosyncratic side to Edinburgh. Experienced guides offer their personal insight into Edinburgh's past, present and future during tours such as Uncover Stories of Crime and Punishment; Real Women of Edinburgh; and The Royal Mile – From Huts to High Rise.

City of Edinburgh Tours (www.cityofedinburghtours.com). Entertaining ghost and history tours ducking through hidden wynds and secret courtyards. Learn Edinburgh's darkest stories – the curious, the uncanny and the terrifying.

Mercat Tours (http://mercattours.com). Various daytime and haunting evening walks through the Old Town's narrow alleyways. Pick from a wide range of history and ghost tours departing from Mercat Cross, High Street;

some depart late in the evening and include a candlelit exploration of the underground vaults of Blair St. It also runs tours to Edinburgh Castle, the Palace of Holyroodhouse and the National Museum of Scotland.

Sandemans Tour (www.newedinburghtours.com). Free city tours every day throughout the day. Meet at 130 High Street; you can book online. Also has specialist paid-for tours.

Bus tours. There are also bus and coach tours to attractions in the city, the surrounding Lothians area and even further north into Scotland. Pick-up points for these are along Waverley Street outside the railway station. Bus tours to outlying areas such as Lowlands, Highlands and St Andrews are also available. One company operating a range of options is Rabbie's (meeting point: Rabbie's bus stop at Waterloo Place; www.rabbies.com). Trips start from £40.

Health and medical care

No general vaccinations are needed for a visit to the UK. Tap water is safe to drink. The National Health Service offers free emergency treatment or first aid to all visitors. Free treatment does not apply to dentistry or to consulting an optician. However, for treatment of a more complicated nature or a pre-existing condition, charges will be made. Citizens of European Union countries are entitled to medical treatment under reciprocal arrangements and should bring their Global Health Insurance Card (GHIC). It is always sensible to take out comprehensive medical insurance for your trip.

The main 24-hour Accident and Emergency hospital is Edinburgh Royal Infirmary, which is in Little France off the Old Dalkeith Road (tel: 536 1000). A 'pay as you go' service provided by experienced doctors can be found at 24 Dundas Street (tel: 0345 1196 049, www.gpplus.com).

A range of over-the-counter drugs are available for everyday ailments. A qualified pharmacist (chemist) will offer advice about the medication you need. There is a dispensing pharmacy open until 7pm at Boots the Chemist (101–3 Princes Street, tel: 225 8331).

For the latest information on how to access the emergency dental services, call the advice line (tel: 536 4800).

Holidays

The following dates are public holidays in the city (generally known as 'bank holidays' in the UK). This means that offices and banks will be closed, but shops and restaurants often remain open. When a bank holiday falls on a Saturday or Sunday, the following Monday will be taken as the official holiday:

Scottish national holidays

New Year, 1–2 January
Good Friday
Easter Monday
May Day, first Monday in May
Spring Holiday, last Monday in May
Christmas Day and Boxing Day, 25–26 December

Additional local holidays in Edinburgh

Edinburgh Spring Holiday, third Monday in April
Victoria Day, third Monday in May
Edinburgh Autumn Holiday, third Monday in Sept

Language

Many place names throughout Scotland are derived from Gaelic names, and words and phrases from the old Scots dialect (called 'Lallans') are still in common use.

Scottish/Gaelic English
auld lang syne days long ago
aye yes
bairn child
ben mountain
bide a wee wait a bit
biggin building
bonny/bonnie pretty
brae hillside

brig bridge
burn stream
cairn pile of stones
ceilidh song and story gathering
clachan hamlet
croft small land-holding
dinna fash yersel' don't get upset
dram measure of whisky
firth estuary
glen valley
haud yer wheesht shut up
inver mouth of river
ken know
knock knoll
kyle strait
lassie girl
links seaside golfcourse
linn waterfall
loch lake
mull promontory
skirl sound of bagpipes
strath river valley
thunderplump thunderstorm
wynd lane

LGBTQ+ travel

The List, which is the club, theatre and cinema guide for Edinburgh and Glasgow, also has a LGBTQ+ section. Support is offered by the LGBT Health and Wellbeing (helpline tel: 0300 123 2523, www.lgbthealth.org.uk), open Tuesday and Wednesday noon–9pm, Thurs and Sun 1–6pm. There are many LGBTQ+ nightlife venues dotted around the city such as *CC Blooms* and *The Regent Bar*.

Lost property

The lost-property department at Waverley Station is on platform 19 (tel: 0330 024 0215). Note that lost property (including that which is left in taxis) found in and around the city centre may be handed in to the police; to report lost property, fill out the relevant form online (www.scotland.police.uk/contact-us/report-lost-property).

Media

The main Scottish newspapers are the *Herald* and the *Scotsman*. Major British daily broadsheet newspapers available around the nation include the *Times*, the *Telegraph*, the *Guardian* and the *Independent*, which all cover world events. Daily tabloid newspapers include the *Sun* and the *Daily Mirror*. A number of newsagents in the city centre sell foreign newspapers.

Five terrestrial television networks operate in Britain: BBC1, BBC2, ITV, Channel 4 and Five, plus numerous digital channels. BBC Scotland produces topical regional programming. Some hotels will provide satellite services such as Sky and CNN. The BBC provides national and local radio services. BBC Radio Scotland can be found on FM 92.4–94.7 and MW 810kHz/370m.

A particularly useful entertainment magazine is *The List*, published every two months and covering music, theatre, cinema, arts and sports in both Edinburgh and Glasgow (www.list.co.uk).

Money

The official currency of Britain is the pound sterling (£); the pound is divided into 100 pence.

Three Scottish banks issue their own notes, which are not, technically, legal tender in England and Wales, although many shops will accept them and English banks will readily change them for you.

Notes are printed in denominations of £5, £10, £20, £50 and £100. Coins are found in denominations of 1p, 2p, 5p, 10p, 20p, 50p, £1 and £2.

Banks and building societies are open Monday–Friday for foreign exchange. There are foreign exchange offices in the Marks and Spencer department store (54 Princes Street) and No1 Currency have branches on

High Street, Queensferry Street and in Waverley Market Shopping Centre. There is also currency exchange available at Edinburgh Airport.

Most banks and building societies will have ATMs that accept international debit cards. Most machines will also dispense cash advances on major credit cards. City centre branches of most banks can be found in and around George Street.

Credit cards are widely accepted for payment in hotels, restaurants and shops, although not always in small guesthouses and B&Bs.

Opening hours

Banks and offices are generally open Monday to Friday from 9am until 5pm; post offices weekdays 9am–5.30pm and Saturday 9am–12.30pm (until 5.30pm for major post offices).

Shops are usually open Monday to Saturday 9am–5.30pm (later opening until 8pm on Thursday) and Sunday 11am–5pm. Hours may be extended during summer.

Restaurants typically open daily noon–2pm and 6–10.30pm, but these hours will differ with the seasons and especially during the Festival. Some restaurants close on Sunday or Monday and some do not open for lunch; others are open all day. Normal opening hours for pubs are Monday to Thursday 11am–midnight, Friday and Saturday until 1am. Normal Sunday hours are 12.30pm–11pm, but extensions until 1am are not uncommon. As in the rest of the UK, smoking is banned in pubs, bars and restaurants.

Police (see also Crime and safety and Emergencies)

British police have a worldwide reputation for friendliness and the ability to give courteous directions. Police uniforms are black and you will see foot patrols (unarmed) operating regular routes in the city. The main police station in Edinburgh is at 2 Gayfield Square. For all emergencies dial **999**.

Public transport (see also Airports)

Buses and trams. Edinburgh has a bus system that travels to all parts of the city as well as out to the coast and the surrounding countryside. The routes are split between several private companies, the main ones being Lothian Buses (www.lothianbuses.com) and First in South East and Central Scotland (www.firstbus.co.uk/south-east-and-central-scotland). The fare for adults is £2 and £1 for children, for any distance. You can pay per trip on the bus (Lothian Buses require exact change) or buy a day ticket (£5 per adult; children pay half, while the good-value family day-ticket is £10.50), although the ticket is not transferable between Lothian and First Bus. A good investment, especially if you're staying away from the centre or want to explore the suburbs, is the £22 'Ridacard' pass allowing a week's unlimited travel on Lothian and tram services (including airport services). A free shuttle service connects the National Galleries of Scotland: National with the Modern One and Two galleries.

Services run from early morning until late into the evening, with several night buses operating on main routes into and out of the city. The main bus station is on Elder Street.

One solitary tram route connects the airport with Murrayfield Stadium, Haymarket, Princes St, St Andrew Square, Leith and Newhaven (www.edinburghtrams.com). Tickets (single £2, day ticket £5 or £12 including the airport) can be bought from vending machines at the tram stops or from the Transport for Edinburgh app. Bus day-tickets are also valid on the tram.

Open-top hop-on, hop-off bus tours are big business in Edinburgh. All cost the same (£18 per person) and depart from Waverley Bridge; see http://edinburghtour.com for information. Try The Regal Tour for access to the harder-to-reach sites like the Royal Yacht *Britannia* and the Royal Botanic Garden Edinburgh. Tickets can be bought at www.edinburghtour.com.

Taxis. Black taxis (like those in London) run all around the city. You can hail them on the street or pick them up at ranks (at Waverley Station and at the west end of East Street). Costs are reasonable – from the city centre to Leith, for example, costs around £10. All taxis are metered, and prices are set by the council; evening and weekend rides cost £1 more than during the week. Companies include Central Taxis (http://taxis-edinburgh.co.uk) and City Cabs (http://citycabs.co.uk). Uber users will have little trouble finding a ride as the city is comprehensively covered.

Trains. Edinburgh's Waverley Station is a major rail hub, providing services to all parts of the UK. Numerous local services are ideal for those who wish to visit other Scottish towns such as North Berwick, Dunbar, Linlithgow, Stirling, St Andrews, Perth and Glasgow.

Telephone

The country code for the United Kingdom is **44**. When dialling from outside the UK, the city code for Edinburgh is **131**; if you are phoning Edinburgh from within the UK, dial **0131**.

Mobile (cell) phone coverage is not as good in Scotland as the rest of the UK, with rural areas particularly neglected by some service providers. Edinburgh, however, has good coverage, including 4G and 5G on most networks. You will need a GSM cellular phone. If visiting from abroad, the cheapest option is to buy a local UK SIM card to use in the GSM phone – incoming calls will be free and local calls inexpensive.

Tickets

Tickets for the Edinburgh International Festival are available from festival offices at The Hub, Castlehill, EH1 2NE (box office tel: 473 2000, www.eif.co.uk).

For Fringe performances contact the Fringe box office, which can be found at 180 High Street (a little below St Giles Cathedral), Edinburgh EH1 1QS (tel: 226 0026, www.edfringe.com).

Military Tattoo tickets can be purchased from the Military Tattoo office at 1–3 Cockburn Street, Edinburgh EH1 1QB (tel: 225 1188, www.edintattoo.co.uk). Telephone and web bookings can be made from early December of the preceding year; early booking is strongly advised.

There is no official central booking agency for theatre performances at other times of the year; tickets can be purchased directly from individual venues (see page 95).

Time zones

The UK runs on Greenwich Mean Time (GMT) in winter and on British Summer Time (BST) in summer. The clocks are put forward one hour on the last Saturday in March, and put back again on the last Saturday in October. The following chart shows the times in various cities during the summer.

San Francisco	New York	**Edinburgh**	Sydney	Auckland
4am	7am	**noon**	9pm	11pm

Tipping

Hotels and restaurants often add a service charge (ten to fifteen percent) to the bill, in which case there is no need to tip. If service has not been satisfactory, this charge may be deducted from the bill. If the charge has not been added to the bill, ten percent is an average tip for satisfactory service. Taxi drivers and hairdressers do not include service charges; a tip of ten percent is normal for satisfactory service.

Toilets

There are public facilities in Waverley Market along Princes Street, at the west end of Princes Street Gardens, Castlehill and Waverley Station (also with showers). There might be a small charge for the use of some facilities. Most tourist attractions will also have public toilet facilities.

Tourist information

Edinburgh's visitor centre has now closed, so your best bet for city information is http://edinburgh.org.

If you require additional information about Edinburgh and Scotland you can also contact VisitScotland (Ocean Point One, 94 Ocean Drive, Edinburgh EH6 6JH, email: info@visitscotland.com, www.visitscotland.com). If you plan to take in other areas in the UK, VisitBritain (www.visitbritain.com) has information on things to do, accommodation, transport and more.

Websites and internet access

Here are a few sites to help you plan your trip. Others can be found in the details for individual attractions, hotels and restaurants in this Guide.

Edinburgh

www.edinburgh.org Comprehensive website all about the city, including some hidden gems

www.edinburghfestivalcity.com Edinburgh's summer festivals

www.list.co.uk The *List* events magazine online

www.edinburghshogmanay.com New-year celebrations

www.ewht.org.uk World Heritage City

www.edinburghguide.com Edinburgh Guide – news, events, info

www.edinburghtourist.co.uk Browse upcoming events, hotels, attractions and more

Youth hostels (see also Accommodation)

The Hostelling Scotland Association central booking office is at 7 Glebe Crescent, Stirling, FK8 2JA (tel: 01786 891 400, central reservations: 0345 2937 7373, www.hostellingscotland.org.uk). You can make reservations directly through the website. Two other booking websites with a good selection of hostels in Edinburgh are www.hostelworld.com and www.edinburghhostels.com.

The flagship *Edinburgh Central Youth Hostel* (9 Haddington Place, tel: 0131 524 2090) has dormitory rooms that start from £19, doubles from £26 per person. *Edinburgh Metro Hostel* is only open in summer, but has a great location off Cowgate and over 300 single rooms (11/2 Robertson's Close, tel: 556 8718). *Castle Rock Hostel* (16 Johnston Terrace, tel: 225 9666, www.castlerockedinburgh.com) is in an ideal central location just beside Edinburgh Castle. Dormitory rooms start from £15.50 per person.

Index

MINI
EDINBURGH

Second Edition 2025

Editor: Joanna Reeves
Updater: Joanna Reeves
Original author: Lindsay Bennett
Picture Manager: Tom Smyth
Cartography Update: Katie Bennett
Layout: Ankur Guha
Production Operations Manager: Katie Bennett
Publishing Technology Manager: Rebeka Davies
Head of Publishing: Sarah Clark
Photography Credits: Alex Knights 63; Bill Wassman/Apa Publications 28; Douglas Macgilvray/Apa Publications 24, 38, 40, 60, 64, 90, 92, 101, 107, 115; iStock 20, 45; Mockford & Bonetti/Apa Publications 12CL, 26, 30, 36, 42, 46, 48, 50, 53, 55, 57, 67, 69, 73, 74, 77, 79, 80, 83, 85, 86, 88, 103, 109, 110; Pete Bennett/Apa Publications 23; Public domain 18BR; Rocco Forte Hotels 14BL; Shutterstock 1, 6, 8, 11, 12TL, 12TR 12CR, 12BL, 12BR, 13T, 13TC, 13CB, 13B, 14CL, 14BR, 16T, 16CL, 16BL, 16BR, 18T, 18CL, 18BL, 25, 33, 34, 59, 71, 84, 97; VisitScotland/Kenny Lam 14T
Cover Credits: Edinburgh floral clock **iStock**

About the author
Joanna Reeves is a Sussex-based travel writer and editor who has updated several UK-based and European Rough Guides, including parts of the Rough Guide to Great Britain and Pocket Rough Guide Edinburgh. She is also the editor of the brand-new Rough Guide to Slow Travel in Europe.

Distribution
UK, Ireland and Europe: Apa Publications (UK) Ltd; mail@roughguides.com
United States and Canada: Two Rivers; ips@ingramcontent.com
Australia and New Zealand: Woodslane; info@woodslane.com.au
Worldwide: Apa Publications (UK) Ltd; mail@roughguides.com

MIX
Paper from responsible sources
FSC® C014138

Special Sales, Content Licensing and CoPublishing
Rough Guides can be purchased in bulk quantities at discounted prices. We can create special editions, personalized jackets and corporate imprints tailored to your needs.
mail@roughguides.com

roughguides.com

EU Representative
LOGOS EUROPE, 9 rue Nicolas Poussin, 17000, LA ROCHELLE, France; Contact@logoseurope.eu; +33 (0) 667937378

Printed by Finidr in Czech Republic

ISBN: 9781835292334

This book was produced using **Typefi** automated publishing software.

A catalogue record for this book is available from the British Library

Contact us
Every effort has been made to ensure that this publication is accurate, free from safety risks, and provides accurate information. However, changes and errors are inevitable. The publisher is not responsible for any resulting loss, inconvenience, injury or safety concerns arising from the use of this book. If you notice any errors, outdated information, or potential safety risks, please send your comments with the subject line "Rough Guide Mini Edinburgh Update" to mail@roughguides.com.